NOISE AND SMOKY BREATH

AN ILLUSTRATED ANTHOLOGY OF
GLASGOW POEMS 1900-1983

Edited by Hamish Whyte

Third Eye Centre (Glasgow) Ltd and
Glasgow District Libraries Publications Board 1983

Noise and Smoky Breath
An Illustrated Anthology of Glasgow Poems 1900-1983
Edited by Hamish Whyte

First published May 1983 in an edition of 75 numbered clothbound copies
signed by main contributors ISBN 0 906474 32 9, 475 clothbound copies
ISBN 0 906474 27 2 and 1550 paperback copies ISBN 0 906474 28 0
Second edition of 2000 copies August 1983

"Noise and Smoky Breath" is subsidised by The Scottish Arts Council

Illustration compilation and selection: Christopher Carrell in association with
George Oliver, Cordelia Oliver and Hamish Whyte
Lay-out and design: Christopher Carrell in association with Pat McKenzie,
Graphic Consultants. Cover design: Pat McKenzie

Published by Third Eye Centre (Glasgow) Ltd and Glasgow District Libraries
Publications Board
Printed by E.F. Peterson, 12 Laygate, South Shields, Tyne and Wear
Distributed by Third Eye Centre, 350 Sauchiehall Street, Glasgow G2 3JD
041-332-7521

Glasgow Art Gallery and Museum (from University Tower), 1905. Annan

EDITOR'S ACKNOWLEDGEMENTS

I should like to thank Duncan Glen for the initial impetus to compile an anthology of Glasgow poems; for useful comment and suggestions along the way, thanks to Alice Bain, Simon Berry, Anne Escott, Joe Fisher, Robin Hamilton, Tom Leonard, Kevin McCarra, Neil McLellan, David Neilson, Alasdair Robertson and Doris Walker; thanks to Tom McGrath for his enthusiasm for the project; special thanks to Edwin Morgan, whose influence on the way we look at and write about Glasgow — particularly as a place to be *celebrated* — cannot be overestimated: his encouragement as the anthology progressed has been of enormous help.

Both Chris Carrell and I would like to thank the lenders of the paintings, prints, drawings and photographs featured in this anthology. Our special thanks are due to Oscar Marzaroli and George Oliver, who were particularly generous in contributing not only a considerable number of their photographs but also valuable advice and encouragement.

Finally, thanks to my wife, Winifred, who has shared this book with me now for long enough.

Hamish Whyte, March 1983

Looking south to the Clyde (from Park Terrace), 1964. Oscar Marzaroli

3

CONTENTS

An old court in the Saltmarket. Pen and ink, 1911. Jessie M. King

GLASGOW

Sing, Poet, 'tis a merry world;
That cottage smoke is rolled and curled
    In sport, that every moss
Is happy, every inch of soil; —
Before *me* runs a road of toil
    With my grave cut across.
Sing, trailing showers and breezy downs —
I know the tragic heart of towns.

City! I am true son of thine;
Ne'er dwelt I where great mornings shine
    Around the bleating pens;
Ne'er by the rivulets I strayed,
And ne'er upon my childhood weighed
    The silence of the glens.
Instead of shores where ocean beats,
I hear the ebb and flow of streets.

Black Labour draws his weary waves,
Into their secret-moaning caves;
    But with the morning light,
That sea again will overflow
With a long weary sound of woe,
    Again to faint in night.
Wave am I in that sea of woes,
Which night and morning, ebbs and flows.

I dwelt within a gloomy court,
Wherein did never sunbeam sport;
    Yet there my heart was stirr'd —
My very blood did dance and thrill,
When on my narrow window-sill,
    Spring lighted like a bird.
Poor flowers — I watched them pine for weeks,
With leaves as pale as human cheeks.

Afar, one summer, I was borne;
Through golden vapours of the morn,
    I heard the hills of sheep:
I trod with a wild ecstasy
The bright fringe of the living sea:
    And on a ruined keep
I sat, and watched an endless plain
Blacken beneath the gloom of rain.

O fair the lightly sprinkled waste,
O'er which a laughing shower has raced!
    O fair the April shoots!
O fair the woods on summer days,
While a blue hyacinthine haze
    Is dreaming round the roots!
In thee, O City! I discern
Another beauty, sad and stern.

Draw thy fierce streams of blinding ore,
Smite on a thousand anvils, roar
    Down to the harbour-bars;
Smoulder in smoky sunsets, flare
On rainy nights, with street and square
    Lie empty to the stars.
From terrace proud to alley base
I know thee as my mother's face.

When sunset bathes thee in his gold,
In wreaths of bronze thy sides are rolled,
    Thy smoke is dusky fire;
And, from the glory round thee poured,
A sunbeam like an angel's sword
    Shivers upon a spire.
Thus have I watched thee, Terror! Dream!
While the blue Night crept up the stream.

The wild Train plunges in the hills,
He shrieks across the midnight rills;
    Streams through the shifting glare,

The roar and flap of foundry fires,
That shake with light the sleeping shires;
      And on the moorlands bare,
He sees afar a crown of light
Hang o'er thee in the hollow night.

At midnight, when thy suburbs lie
As silent as a noonday sky,
      When larks with heat are mute,
I love to linger on thy bridge,
All lonely as a mountain ridge,
      Disturbed but with my foot;
While the black lazy stream beneath,
Steals from its far-off wilds of heath.

And through thy heart, as through a dream,
Flows on that black disdainful stream;
      All scornfully it flows,
Between the huddled gloom of masts,
Silent as pines unvexed by blasts —
      'Tween lamps in streaming rows.
O wondrous sight! O stream of dread!
O long dark river of the dead!

Afar, the banner of the year
Unfurls: but dimly prisoned here,
      'Tis only when I greet
A dropt rose lying in my way,
A butterfly that flutters gay
      Athwart the noisy street,
I know the happy Summer smiles
Around thy suburbs, miles on miles.

'T were neither paean now, nor dirge,
The flash and thunder of the surge
      On flat sands wide and bare;
No haunting joy or anguish dwells
In the green light of sunny dells,
      Or in the starry air.

Alike to me the desert flower,
The rainbow laughing o'er the shower.

While o'er thy walls the darkness sails,
I lean against the churchyard rails;
    Up in the midnight towers
The belfried spire, the street is dead,
I hear in silence over head
    The clang of iron hours:
It moves me not — I know her tomb
Is yonder in the shapeless gloom.

All raptures of this mortal breath,
Solemnities of life and death,
    Dwell in thy noise alone:
Of me thou hast become a part —
Some kindred with my human heart
    Lives in thy streets of stone;
For we have been familiar more
Than galley-slave and weary oar.

The beech is dipped in wine, the shower
Is burnished; on the swinging flower
    The latest bee doth sit.
The low sun stares through dust of gold,
And o'er the darkening heath and wold
    The large ghost-moth doth flit.
In every orchard Autumn stands,
With apples in his golden hands.

But all these sights and sounds are strange;
Then wherefore from thee should I range?
    Thou hast my kith and kin:
My childhood, youth, and manhood brave;
Thou hast that unforgotten grave
    Within thy central din.
A sacredness of love and death
Dwells in thy noise and smoky breath.

Alexander Smith, 1857

INTRODUCTION

"In the many descriptions of Glasgow it seems to have been the last thing dreamt of to consider the town as a place of inspiration for poets." (Eyre-Todd, *The Glasgow Poets*, 1903) From McUre to Oakley and Smollett to McIlvanney Glasgow has been recorded and dissected by historian and novelist alike; it is time the poet's Glasgow had its due: according to S.G. Checkland in *The Upas Tree* (1976) "among the few groups in society who can interpret the social elements of Glasgow to themselves and to one another are its folksingers and its poets." At the very least these lyrical sociologists provide another way of seeing the city.

This collection, as far as I know, is the first anthology of poems *about* Glasgow. There have been a few attempts this century to bring together in book form the work of Glasgow poets: Eyre-Todd's *The Glasgow Poets* (1903), the Glasgow Ballad Club collections (1924, 1952), *A Sense of Belonging* (1977), and, most recently, Geddes Thomson's *Identities* (1981) which also included prose and drama and covered the West of Scotland, not just Glasgow. The emphasis in most of these collections has usually been on the work of the poets in general rather than concentrating on their response to one particular area, although the sense of place is never excluded. Poets have written about Glasgow since at least 1685 ("And blushing roses grow into thy fields" — John Barclay), but the good poems were few and far between — such as those of Dougal Graham, John Mayne, or Alexander Smith (all in Eyre-Todd). The industrial revolution for all its effect on Glasgow provoked little poetry. The later 19th century *Clydeside Litterateurs* "showed little real interest in their city" (Checkland) and in 1935 William Montgomerie asked, "Why were all the poets dumb?" Hugh MacDiarmid, at least, was not silent, as witness his passionate pessimistic poems of the '30s and '40s, "In the Slums of Glasgow", "In Glasgow Today" etc., but the rest were probably writing novels, if they were writing. The city inspired fiction rather than poetry.

However, in the last twenty years increasing numbers of poems about Glasgow have appeared, along with the emergence of a recognisable group of Glasgow poets — not a "school" as has been claimed, but a group of individual poets with roots in Glasgow or close connections with the city which, allied to an outlook distinctly non-parochial, are revealed in their work: poets such as Edwin Morgan, Stephen Mulrine, Tom McGrath, Tom Leonard, Alan Spence, Liz Lochhead. It may have had something to do with the gradual destruction — "the desperate throes of renewal" (Edwin Morgan) — of the old fabric of Glasgow. As the city has been altered — in some parts out of all recognition — there has been a growing interest in its past as well as its future, seen in the number of local newspapers, tenants associations, amenity societies, local history clubs — it would seem the changing city demanded to be improved, preserved, recorded, depending on the various viewpoints. And the poets were no longer dumb. In fact, the sheer number of Glasgow poems produced in the '60s and '70s is astonishing, although it perhaps became fashionable to write a

"Glasgow" poem, and some were hardly more than "a recital of street names with a description of a few well known buildings thrown in" (John Cockburn on Glasgow fiction, 1933) whose greatest appreciation was merely a recognition of familiar places. This may be more excusable now, with so little of old Glasgow remaining. Glasgow has too much to be nostalgic about. Only recently, for example, the Underground (the "Subway") was modernised and Edwin Morgan's Madame Emé (Glasgow Sonnet viii) vanished almost overnight. As for the poems, mainly love poems, which on the face of it have no obvious concern with place but have been labelled by the poets "Glasgow" — e.g. Robin Hamilton's "The Girl I Met in Byres Road" and Edwin Morgan's "In Glasgow" — could they have been set elsewhere? Glasgow is surely as potent a symbol as, say, Stonehenge.

In view of the wealth of modern Glasgow verse this anthology is intended to represent, some sort of division by subject seemed desirable: Glaswegians, the Clyde, songs, violence, etc. This indeed was the original intention, and the poems were arranged in groups with the hope that they would (in the words of the editors of *New Poems 1955*) "speak to each other, exchanging . . . ideas, occasionally answering each other back." However, many of the categories overlapped, some poems were equally at home in more than one section, Glasgow, in fact, seemed unclassifiable in the last resort, defying definition. The arrangement finally decided on is a chronological one, which has the advantage of reflecting the growth of interest in Glasgow as a theme for poetry and the different approaches made to it this century; also, perhaps more than a subject arrangement does, it points up the contrasts and mixtures of Glasgow life. Such as the Glasgow toughness: the hardmen, Tom Leonard's "Cowboyz", greeting over a dead speug in the gutter (to paraphrase Chandler); and the heroic generosity that can turn without warning to blind hostility. Nor has kailyardery been avoided — couthieness and sentimentality are very much a part of the Glaswegian character (is Country and Western today's Whistle Binkie?). This contradiction (love/hate, violence/sentimentality) is expressed in Nicol Cunningham's "Hey Yoo":

> "Ye think it's hate, pal, but ye're wrang . . .
> any minute noo yoo an me's
> goin tae get lyrical."

The order of the poems is only roughly chronological: either according to the date of composition, where known, or date of first publication — or, in some cases, first significant appearance. The notes should help to clarify some of these points.

About a quarter of the poems included are written in Glasgow patois ("dialect" poems) and illustrate the extent of the experimentation. Tom Leonard's success in this medium has tended to overshadow the others — from Ian Hamilton Finlay's pioneering "Glasgow Beasts, an a Burd" of 1961 to David Neilson's recent versions of Catullus. Simon Berry has suggested that the use of dialect could indicate a desire to experiment with phonetics or to create a tension between medium and content as well as to indulge in referential humour often of a rather pointless kind, or to establish the "street-name" easy associations of hand-me-down nostalgia. On the other hand: as Belli is made to say in Anthony Burgess's *Abba Abba:* "What in God's name is the difference between a language and a dialect? I'll tell you. A language waves flags and is blown up by politicians. A dialect keeps to things, things, street smells and street noises, life."

The poems chosen are not necessarily those I consider the best poems about Glasgow — these rival the great Glasgow novel in scarcity — but ones which contribute each in its way to a picture of the city (although I would hope the best *are* included). Some demand to be included, of course, those which have passed into Glasgow mythology: "The Coming of the Wee Malkies", "The Good Thief", "The Jeely Piece Song", "Cod Liver Oil and Orange Juice" (all in Glasgow "dialect"). There are humorous, even pawky, poems to counter-balance the poems of the dark side of Glasgow; and, following the Riding and Graves definition of a true anthology as a historical rescue-work, poems which might have languished forgotten in back numbers of small magazines and defunct journals (fitting graves some might argue) and which are worth reviving (such as "Night Pillion" by Edwin Morgan and "Monster" by Archie McCallum). Some of the work, for example that of Leonard, Lochhead, and Morgan will be already familiar, but no apology is offered for presenting it again beyond its appropriateness in this collection. There are no doubt bad poems in the anthology and good ones missed out — and plenty to be quarrelled with, not least among Glaswegians themselves: "It's as much in [their] nature to heckle as it is in the nature of the city to awaken in every fresh observer a rediscovery of all its clichés." (Hugh MacDiarmid) So I wish the reader an interesting journey through the clichés of twentieth century poetical Glasgow, "from the hilarious to the horrific with all stages in between." (Edwin Morgan)

Hamish Whyte, March 1983

Celtic supporters; Celtic v Rangers Cup Final, Hampden Park, 1963. Oscar Marzaroli

13

GLASGOW THROUGH ARTISTS' EYES

Twenty-odd years ago the architect and broadcaster, Ian Nairn, paid a visit to Glasgow for a Third Programme series on Britain's Changing Towns. At the time, as an Englishman dependent mostly on hearsay and legend for his ideas about Glasgow, he freely admitted that the reality had come as a surprise, and a favourable one at that. "I expected", he said, "to find something like a vast Scottish mixture of the worst of Leicester and Liverpool, with a few outstanding buildings embedded in it. Instead, I found what is without doubt the most friendly of Britain's big cities, and the most dignified and coherent as well — in looks, more like the best parts of Boston and Philadelphia than anywhere in Britain. There are, indeed, the slums, and their consequences . . . but there is so much else as well; and it is usually only the slums that receive the publicity."

That was back in 1960, and it has to be said that the intervening years have brought significant changes; by no means always for the better. Some of the visual coherence Nairn found so unexpected and impressive has gone forever under the bulldozers — though, happily, not all by any means. But the media concentration, much to Glasgow's disservice in the world's eyes, remains fixed relentlessly on the dereliction and the deprivation with its consequent drunkenness and crime — not really any worse in Glasgow than in any comparable British city.

To the seeing eye, the place which was for many years the "second city of the Empire", and the sight of which charmed the eighteenth century writer Daniel Defoe into calling it "the cleanest and beautifullest, and best built city in Britain, London excepted", is still a place of abiding interest visually, whether it is in the play of light and the wonderful climatic transience over its substantial masonry, across its sky and riverscape; or in the strange, oddly exciting contrasts of new and older elements as the inner city undergoes its traumatic changes.

Even the process of demolition — not new, incidentally, to our own century: the splendidly atmospheric photographs of Thomas Annan of old Glasgow closes, were made as a record before the Victorian demolishers moved in — has its dramatic as well as its sad side. And the people of Clydeside, polyglot and extrovert, jovial and anarchic by nature, would seem to offer endless subject matter, not least in their street life, to any artist with a primary interest in the human situation.

Yet, oddly enough, Glasgow's painters have often turned their backs on this wealth of subject matter on their doorstep. Muirhead Bone, that assiduous recorder of the local topography, once expressed his astonishment that, even in their heyday, not one of the Glasgow Boys responded with any enthusiasm to what he himself clearly found so stimulating — the intimate street scene and the wider cityscape. Bone, of course, was a nonpareil in his own field, and he left a marvellous record of "how it looked then" — indeed, of how it still looks on certain days in those places which have suffered less physical change than most.

James Miller and Ian Fleming share the linear gift which seems to have blessed a number of Glasgow artists (in the next generation Alasdair Gray and Willie Rodger are notable examples) and, by coincidence, both Miller and Fleming have lived through, and been inspired to record, scenes of wartime destruction. It was a war, too, which brought Stanley Spencer north to Glasgow in the early 1940s to make an official record (at the suggestion, incidentally, of Sir Muirhead Bone, then helping to organise the work of the war artists) of shipbuilding activity on Clydeside.

Sometimes it takes an incomer to penetrate beyond received ideas of sordidness and dereliction; even when, as in the case of J.D. Fergusson, the verdurous aspects of Kelvinside are seen through Cézanne-enlightened eyes. Yet it *is* a fact that Glasgow's acreage of greenery within its boundaries is greater in proportion to its size than any other British city.

And certain places, not so countrified, have always attracted the painter's eye — the canal, for example, on the north side of the city, because of its romantic, alien aspect, more like northern Europe than familiar Glasgow. Bet Low and Tom Macdonald are among those who, in their early work, recorded the scene around the canal basin at Port Dundas.

This book, of course, is not primarily about pictures. The poems came first in its conception and many of those are in any case, so alive with their own verbal imagery that they need no illustration. But one poem, by Edwin Morgan, actually sprang from his own keen appreciation of a painter's response to the sight of slum children playing on the pavement in Townhead. Joan Eardley it was who, most consistently, found apt equivalents in paint for the colourfully disintegrating environment and the noisy juvenile street life around her east end studio during the 'forties and early 'fifties. Eardley's dilapidated tenements are as full of character as are the urchins in her drawings and paintings, busily scribbling on walls and pavingstones, or sharing private jokes and animosities.

So the pictures in this book are not mere illustrations, whether they are drawings, paintings, prints, or the photographic images which are, increasingly, taking over in this age of the ubiquitous camera, and the best of which reveal the true artist's "seeing eye".

In this field one name predominates: no other concern or individual has had a closer or longer association with photography in this place, and for anyone seeking early pictures the starting place, inevitably, must be the West Campbell Street premises of T. & R. Annan & Sons. Despite the activities of Annan photographers over the years, however, photographic coverage of the look and the life of this great city is nowhere near as comprehensive as one could wish. To date there has been no detailed study of its structure and its street life of the kind carried out with such sensitivity and understanding by Berenice Abbott in New York in the nineteen thirties, for example, or the less ambitious but pictorially more exciting survey made there during the 'forties by Andreas 15

Feininger. Nor has there been any systematic recording of its remarkably cosmopolitan population.

Fortunately, however, some individuals have been quietly active in recent years, catching with their cameras some record of a period of vast visual change. From them and from the Annan archives a representative selection of photographs of the look and the life of Glasgow has been made for this book — a sampling of what it might be possible to develop on a much larger scale at some future time. But that's another story.

Meanwhile, in this book, it will be obvious that not everything relates directly to the poems. Indeed the majority may rather offer a complementary extension to the poet's view which, with notable exceptions seems to focus doggedly (and, in the case of one of the greatest, Hugh MacDiarmid, with a disgust which, to me, suggests a kind of transference from self to surroundings) on the seamy, sordid side of Glasgow life, to the exclusion of the vitality, the truculent cheerfulness, the talent for comedy, for histrionics (think of all the Glasgow comedians of genius, from Tommy Lorne and Lex McLean to Billy Connolly) and the sheer warmth of character which, as Ian Nairn discovered, epitomises this once great western seaport, even in its decline. It is decline, moreover, which is only so in commercial terms: Glasgow is still, as it always was, the centre of musical activity in Scotland. Here is the home of the first (and still the Scottish National) orchestra; the opera and the ballet; the colleges of music and drama; the only internationally known theatre company in Scotland; and an arts centre which, for variety, standard and popularity right across the board — for Glasgow is less class-ridden than most large cities — can vie with any in Britain. No mean city, indeed!

Cordelia Oliver, March 1983

Last Night at the Proms: Sir Alexander Gibson and the Scottish National Orchestra, Kelvin Hall, 1982. Oscar Marzaroli

16

Behind a Gallowgate tenement, looking east. Pen and ink, 1977. Alasdair Gray

Woman at kitchen sink. Pen and wash, c1943. Harry Keir　　17

The 1901 Glasgow International Exhibition. Annan

18 The Clyde from Sailors' Home, Broomielaw, c1900. Annan

EXHIBITION ODE, No. III

HAIL, this glorious enterprise,
Open now to all our eyes,
Where are treasures rich and rare,
Crowned with beauty past compare!

Here Invention's power we find
In the triumphs of the mind,
Here the fruits of Industry,
Brought to us from o'er the sea!

Nature here her produce pours,
Which she brings from foreign shores,
While the handicraft of man
In perfection we may scan.

Long may Commerce flourish still
In our midst, and may good-will
Be maintained o'er all the world,
And the flag of Peace unfurled!

Long may Glasgow's trade increase
With the advent of sweet Peace,
And our efforts firmly bind
Hearts and hands of all mankind!

Middlemass Brown, 1901

ODE TO THE CLYDE

Hail, great black-bosomed mother of our city,
   Whose odoriferous breath offends the earth,
Whose cats and puppy dogs excite our pity,
   As they sail past with aldermanic girth!
No salmon hast thou in thy jet-black waters,
   Save what is adhering to the tins.
Thus thy adorers — Govan's lovely daughters —
   Adorn thy shrine with offerings for their sins.

19

No sedges check thy flow, nor water lily;
   Thy banks are unadorned with hip or haw,
'Cos why? — now, don't pretend you're *really* silly,
   There ain't no lilies at the Broomielaw.
MacBrayne defiles thy face with coaly sweepings,
   Into thy lap the tar expectorates;
The "Caledonia's" cook his galley heapings
   Casts in thy face as if at one he hates.

Yet art thou great. Though strangers hold their noses
   When sailing down to Rothesay at the Fair,
Thy exiled sons would barter tons of roses
   To scent thy sweetness on the desert air.

Charles J. Kirk, 1910

20   Trams on Jamaica Bridge, c.1924. Annan

GLASGOW TYPES

No. I The car conductor

Ach! I'd raither be a cairter wi'
    a horse an' coal briquettes,
Or an interferin' polis catchin'
    bookies makin' bets,
But tae staun' a' day collectin'
    maiks an' gettin' tons o' lup
Frae auld wives an' cheeky wee-
    men — man, it fairly feeds me up!

Wur first run in the mornin's wi'
    a lot o' silly goats,
Doon tae Yoker an' Kilpatrick,
    whaur they mak' the iron boats;
They smoke an' spit an' argy wha
    is likely tae get in,
Exceptin' when they're narkin' ower
    the heid o' Jimmy Quin.

But they're angels, bloomin' angels, compared wi'
    whit I get
In the efternune an' evenin — mair pertikler if it's
    wet;
Auld wives oot daein' shoppin', an' as nesty as can be,
When they're cairret on tae Partick an' them wantin'
    Polmadie.

Ach! I'd raither be a cairter wi' a horse an' coal
    briquettes,
Or an interferin' polis catchin' bookies makin' bets,
For I'm seik o' cheeky weemen, wi' their impidence
    an' fuss,
An' the Corporation, they can — richt, Wull. Here's
    the terminus.

No. II The four-wheeler

I'll put ma twa feet through yer biler,
    Ay, you wi' the rid motor caur!
Scarin' ma' horse wi' yir hooter,
    An' spilin' ma cab wi' yir glaur.
An' the stink o' yir smoke's somethin' awfu';
    Div ye feed yir auld taxi wi' taur?

Nyafs like you are the ruin o' Glesga',
    'Twould mak' even an angel feel sair,
Wi' yir flag stickin' oot o' yir shouther
    Tae show that you're wantin' a fare.
An' the toffs say, "Awa', wi' yir growler,
    A taxi's the thing I prefer."

It's weeks since I've earned a curdy.
    I canna afford even beer
Since you wi' yir auld hurdy-gurdy
    Came an' ended ma honest career.
An' Wull's ribs are like girds on a barrel,
    You could strike matches on them gey near.

May yir sparkin' plugs stick in yir thrapple,
    Broken bottles stick intae each tyre,
May yir petrol tank leak till its empty,
    An' spile a' yir chance o' a hire.
An' I hope that a spark frae yir ingin
    will set the whole d — d thing on fire.

22

No. III The flapper

I'm fair run aff ma tootsies in the tea-
    shop whaur I work,
An' between the boss an' customers
    I'm mad as ony Turk.
But when the shops are closin', an' the
    nicht begins tae fall,
I put ma glad rags on an' seek the
    Rue de Sauchiehall.

I'm an expert wi' the glad eye, an' ma
    Merry Widda hat
Is quite the latest *chapeau* (it's French
    menus that did that!),
An' ye'd never think tae hear me that
    I lived sae near the slums
When I speak aboot pa's motor an'
    oor yacht wi' twa rid lums.

I think roller skatin's jolly (when ye get some fool tae
    pey),
But I never tak' a second look at them that smokes
    the cley.
Ma best boy's name is Bertie, an' he lives in
    Pollokshields,
An' he gives me everythin' I ask (he's greener than
    the fields).

I'm awfu' fond o' music-halls, I visit fower each
    week,
But I canna staun the opera, yon singin' mak's me
    seik.
"All the nice girls love a sailor," or a song wi'
    somethin' light
Is the sort o' song I — (Hullo, Bertie! Whaur we
    gaun the night?)

No. IV The engineer

The Shwe Dagon's a bonnie kirk a'
    set wi' rubies braw,
Wee twisty golden minarets, ye coodna
    coont them a';
They say yon ugly idol's e'en wid buy
    the P. and O.,
Man, I'd raither hae the auld Tron
    Kirk; av coorse, *ma* tastes are low.

Ye mind yon army chap we carried
    tae Bombay last year?
He used tae sit an' talk wi' me among
    the engines here,
Aboot Simla, an' the polo, an' the
    splendid mountain air,
Man, *he'd* never slept in Skeoch Wid
    in Rothesay at the Fair.

Last trip we broke oor record, an' the owners peyed
    up well,
So me an' Mac did table d'hôte in thon Bombay hotel,
There were fifteen different courses, but Mac whispered
    ower tae me,
"Man, I'd swap it a' for ham an' eggs an' some o'
    Lockhart's tea!"

Ay, Glesca mud's no' jist as nice as India's coral
    strand
(Ye'd hae tae dredger gey faur doon afore ye came tae
    sand),
But yir eyes look kind o' happy, an' yir breist begins
    tae swell
When you're sailin' up by Greenock, an' — gosh, there's
    the "stand-by" bell!

No. V The barmaid

When a fella calls me Tottie, I put on
    an air that's haughty
If his hair ain't brilliantiny an' his
    ties the latest shade,
But I'm always called Salome by the
    nuts who really know me,
When they ask for Johnnie Walker
    and a little lemonade.

When a fella asks for lager, with a glance I make him
    stagger,
Interruptin' me an' Bertie in a gentle tête-à-tête;
An' if he should turn crusty, well, he gets his lager —
    musty
From the cask I keep for customers who haven't long
    to wait.

Though my years are somewhat mellow, yet peroxide
    keeps hair yellow,
An' I look so sweet an' girlish when I'm skatin' at
    the rink.
When in Sauchiehall I'm walkin', showin' just a little
    stockin',
Well, you'd never dream I spent my days a-moppin'
    up the zinc.

So when Death has caught us bendin', an' there ain't
    no more coin spendin',
When we're gathered to the regions where there's
    neither flasks or taps,
You will find me there, I hope, handin' out the grateful
    dope
When you're roostin' up in heaven — or the other place
    perhaps.

Charles J. Kirk, 1910

25

I BELONG TO GLASGOW (Chorus)

I belong to Glasgow
Dear Old Glasgow town!
But what's the matter with Glasgow?
For it's going round and round.
I'm only a common old working chap,
As anyone can see,
But when I get a couple of drinks on a Saturday,
Glasgow belongs to me.

Will Fyffe, 1921

Victoria Bar. Pen and wash, c1943. Harry Keir

NUNS IN GORDON STREET

Sun and wind dropt happily down
The caverned canyons of the town.

In Gordon Street young girls came
In summer dresses, flame upon flame,

And business men went swiftly by,
Sifting the colours with one eye;

And newsboys shouted, "Irish War!"
Motors hooted, and clanged each car!

I saw the street aflame with life,
With beauty, joy, with dread, with strife, —

Then, o'er the way, from auction room
To footware store, a cloak of gloom,

Two cloaks of gloom, three, four I saw:
It was four nuns, of austere law

The symbols, spiritual brides
Of Jesus whom the world derides.

I saw them walk with careful feet;
White linen pale grey cheeks did meet

When breezes stirred, and eight grey eyes
Shed beams of dawnlike grey surprise.

I gazed, and it was strange to see
These walk the living street with me,

With me, with you, with all mankind
In this stern age of powerful mind

When atoms break, and old laws sway,
And God's a little bird astray,

A little bird with broken wing
Through empty hearts a-wandering!

And while I thought, a great wind rose
And ran between the building rows

And grasped the people one by one
And threw them, till their life was done;

And following the wind there came
From heaven's mouth a cloud of flame

That streamed along the building tops
Till highest flats and lowest shops

Were furnaces of fire; and then
(Too great a sight for mortal ken)

I swooned; and, waking 'midst deep peace,
It seemed that earthly Time's increase

Beyond all count had gone; for there
Were neither buildings rising fair

And bright in sunny Gordon Street
Nor men's nor women's eyes to meet,

But ruins only, grey with age,
And thorns and weeds on pilgrimage.

And I was not alone therein!
I trembled, as I were a sin

Discovered by the eyes of God!
Yea! I saw, walking the sod,

Treading the grass with printless feet,
Throwing no shadow earth to meet,

Breathing the air with unmoved breasts,
The four pale nuns, on strange, strange hests!

What sought these visionary nuns?
Human voices? laughter of sons

And daughters in a happy house?
Marriage music? youth's carouse?

What were ye seeking, O virgins cold,
Weary of wandering, phantoms old?

28   **William Jeffrey, 1923**

Gordon Street. Pencil, 1910. Sir Muirhead Bone

29

THE YAIRDS

I've wrocht amang them, man and boy, for mair nor fifty year,
I canna bear to quit them yet noo that I'm auld an' sere,
The Yairds is just the life o' me, the music's in my bluid
O' hammers striking strong an true on rivets loweing rid;
I'm auld, I ken, but, Goad be thank'd! I hivna lost my pride
In honest wark on bonny boats that's built upon the Clyde.

Frae Broomielaw to Kempoch Point I ken them every yin,
I kent them when I was a wean when I could hardly rin;
I kent them as a rivet boy, I kent them in my prime,
An' tho' there's been an unco wheen o' chainges in my time,
Yet still it's aye a bonny sicht to see them in their pride,
Wi' "weys" laid doun an' some big boat a' ready for the tide.

30   *Clyde shipyard being rebuilt.* Lithograph, 1917-1918. Sir Muirhead Bone

It's graun' to see the boats grow up frae keel to upper strake,
An' ken it's a' guid honest wark an' no' an unce o' fake;
It's graun' to see the muckle frames staun' up like leafless trees,
To hear the clang o' plates an' see the rivet furnace bleeze,
To see the bonny boats tak' shape just like a leevin' thing,
Eh, man, but it's a bonny sicht an' fit to please a king.

I've helped to build a wheen o' them in mony a different yaird,
Frae barges up to battleships the Empire for to guaird,
An' eh, the names I could reca' o' men noo passed awa
Wha planned and built the boats lang syne, aye trig and strang and braw.
The men hae gane, but left ahint a legacy o' fame,
For honest wark an' bonny boats that gied the Clyde its name.

Tod an' McGregor, Napier tae, John Elder, an' the Scott's,
Wi' auld Wull Fyfe, awa doun bye, aye buildin' bonny yachts,
The "Limited," an' Simonses, the Tamson's at Clydebank
(That's noo John Broon's), an' Stephens whaur the puir *Daphne* sank,
An' Caird's, an' Connel's, Barclay Curles, an' Russell, an' Dunlop,
An' Fairfield, Beardmore's, Tammy Seath's — I've wrocht in every shop.

Ye'll hear it said the "Black Squad" drink an' break their time forbye,
Weel I jaloose we hae oor fauts — jist let the jaw gang by;
But this I'll say that, gin we drink an' break oor time as weel,
Wi' a' oor fauts, by Goad! we ken jist hoo to lay a keel,
An' build a boat that nane can beat in a' the warld beside,
The best o' wark, the bonniest boats aye come frae oot the Clyde.

John F. Fergus, 1924

GLESCA'

Hech, sirs! but I'm wabbit, I'm back frae the toon;
I ha'ena dune pechin' — jist let me sit doon.
I'm for nae mair o' Glesca', an' that's shair as death;
But ye'll hear a' ma crack when I've gotten ma breath.
Eh, man, I'm fairfochen! Is't drouthy I look?
Aye, weel could I dae wi' a waucht o' soor-dook.

Dod aye! I'm fair dunner't, an' think it nae shame;
It's an awfu' place, Glesca'; I'm gled tae get hame.

For mony a year noo we've ettled tae gang;
An' noo that we've dune it I think we were wrang;
But we're spared tae come back tae the place that we ken,
An' the weys we're aquant wi' up here in the glen.
We stertit this mornin', John, me an' the weans —
It's an unchancy business this trevellin' in trains —
Ilka station we stopp'd at John speir'd for its name;
But when we reach'd Glesca' I wish'd we were hame.

For the reek o' the toon rase frae thoosan's o' lums;
An' the roar o' its streets was like duntin' on drums.
What a thrangity! folk gaed in droves thick as craws;
An' ye couldna see naethin' for hooses an' wa's.
I cried: "Michty me! this is somethin' extr'ornar'!"
John stopp'd oot gey bauldly, said, "Naethin' byor'nar'."
Wi' a wean in ilk oxter, ma he'rt in ma wame,
 I followed him sighin': "I wish we were hame."

When John cried: "Yon ill-lookin' chiel wi' the slooch
That stottit agin me has rypit ma pooch!"
Ma he'rt gi'ed a stoun' an' ma heid gi'ed a whirl.
Then a big, feckless polisman birl't on his birl,
An' syne wi' anither gaed daunerin' roon' —
Ye can lippen tae naebody there in the toon.
Then John cried: "Ma siller's a' richt, I'm tae blame —
It's here in ma breeks. Dod! I wish we were hame."

I'm wae for puir bodies that bide in thae streets:
Nae gress for their coo or for bleachin' o' sheets;
An' the caurs an' the wa's are a' cover'd wi' bills,
Sic as "Keep tae the left" an' "Try Thingummy's pills";
An' the folk ha'e tae thole a' thae fashious instructions.
Faith! try it in Kippen and there would be ructions!
I said this tae John an' he thocht jist the same:
"It's a dowie place, Glesca', I wish we were hame."

We speir'd for a place tae get somethin' tae eat,
An' sune were direc'it tae ane ower the street.
Sae we joukit twa lorries, three caurs an' a hearse,
An' syne we collec' it in-by nane the warse.
I order'd some milk an' twa-three cogs o' brose;
But the besom wha sair'd us jist turn'd up her nose.
"Is that Glesca' mainners?" says I, "Lass, think shame,
We ken better in Kippen." An' syne we cam' hame.

W. D. Cocker, 1925

IN GLASGOW

(For F.G. Scott)

How can I but be fearful,
Who know not what I do
More than did they whose labours
We owe this chaos to?

I'd rather cease from singing,
Than make by singing wrong
An ultimate Cowcaddens,
Or Gorbals of a song.

I'll call myself a poet,
And know that I am fit
When my eyes make glass of Glasgow,
And foresee the end of it!

Hugh MacDiarmid, 1925

O.M.

GLASGOW STREET

Out of this ugliness may come
    some day so beautiful a flower
    that men will wonder at that hour
remembering smoke and flowerless slum
    and ask
        glimpsing the agony
    of the slaves who wrestle to be free
"But why were all the poets dumb?"

William Montgomerie, 1933

"The women talk, tea-drinking by the fire"

The women talk, tea-drinking by the fire
    In the back parlour. The rose afternoon
Stiffens out in the street to fog and mire.
    The blood-red bullying West confronts the moon.

The house-tops, sharpening, saw into the sky.
    Factory sirens wail and Rest is born,
A clockwork centipede that lumbering by
    Decorates heaven with silhouettes of horn.

Incandescent burners' arctic glare
  Strikes dead a thousand families as they sit
At high tea in the tenements. The air
  Takes at the tidal corner of the street

The hundred-horse-power pub's wave-shouldering boom
  And thickened voices babbling Judgement Day.
At the big house the Owner waits his doom
  While his Rhine-maiden daughters sit and play

Wagner and Strauss. Beneath the railway bridge
  In patient waxwork line the lovers stand.
Venus weeps overhead. Poised on the ridge
  The unemployed regard the Promised Land.

Edwin Muir, 1935

GLASGOW, 1960

Returning to Glasgow after long exile
Nothing seemed to me to have changed its style.
Buses and trams all labelled "To Ibrox"
Swung past packed tight as they'd hold with folks.
Football match, I concluded, but just to make sure
I asked; and the man looked at me fell dour,
Then said, "Where in God's name are *you* frae, sir?
It'll be a record gate, but the cause o' the stir
Is a debate on 'la loi de l'effort converti'
Between Professor MacFadyen and a Spainish pairty."
I gasped. The newsboys came running along,
"Special! Turkish Poet's Abstruse New Song.
Scottish Authors' Opinions" — and, holy snakes,
I saw the edition sell like hot cakes!

Hugh MacDiarmid, 1935

THE CITY CEMETERY

(Written in Glasgow)

There are open railings and walls
and black earth and no trees and no grass
and wooden benches where old people sit
the whole afternoon without speaking.
All around there are tenements and shops.
The children play in streets and the trains
rattle past the graves. It is a poor district.

As if patching-up some piece of grey material, rain
-sodden rags hang across the windows.
The writing on the tombstones is unreadable, and anyway
for the last two hundred years they have been burying not men
but corpses without friends even to forget them, dead
secrets. But when the sun blazes for those few days
around June, surely the old bones down there feel something.

No leaf, no bird. Nothing but stone. Earth.
Is Hell like this? Pain and more pain, clamour,
misery, a chill that seeps everywhere freezing
everything; and the dead are not left in peace,
for life goes about its business here like a prostitute
who works only under the cover of darkness.

When the dirty evening twilight smears the sky
and the factory smoke falls back down
as grey ash, people are shouting in the pubs;
and then a train passes,
its echoes stretching the sounds like a trumpet's snarl.

— But not for Judgement Day. You have no names now,
so be at peace; if you can sleep, then sleep.
For even God may be forgetting you.

Luis Cernuda, 1940

36 *Translated by Ronald Butlin*

from GLASGOW

"It is not every poet who has the inner authority for remarking
that Glasgow contains a million slaves."

The Listener

"Nothing in Nature is unserviceable,
No not even inutility itself.
Is, then, for nought dishonesty in being?
And, if it be sometimes of forced use,
Wherein more urgent than in saving nations?"

Marston

Wagner might call Berlin a city
Of sordid spaces and pretensions to greatness;
Berlioz write down Paris "the infernal city
That thinks itself the home of art" — Glasgow
(Though Cazamian praises its *originalité puissante*
— A phrase I too might use even as Villon in his hymn
To the Blessed Virgin the triple invocation to Dian-Hecate!)
Thinks nothing, and is content to be
Just what it is, not caring or knowing what.
Crowded with grundformen, incommunicable as handwriting,
It is beyond all human knowing indeed,
And that's the only knowing there is, alas!

"Let a Colgate smile get you out of it."

The houses are Glasgow, not the people — these
(Their characters all shaded to suit their environment.
Life doesn't *take* here).
Are simply the food the houses live and grow on
Endlessly, drawing from them their vulgarity
And pettiness and darkness of spirit
Τυφλος τα τ'ῶτα τον τε νουν τ'ὀμματ' εἰ! [1]
— Gorgonising the mindless generations,
Turning them all into filthy property,
Apt as the Karaunas by diabolic arts
To produce darkness and obscure the light of day.

37

To see and hear the clock in Glasgow's horrible,
Like seeing a dead man's watch, still going though he's dead.[2]
Every thing is dead except stupidity here,
Smelling like the dissection of bad innards
Or like the cold stench of ashes and foul water.

Where have I seen a human being looking
As Glasgow looked this gin-clear evening — with face and fingers
A cadaverous blue, hand-clasp slimy and cold
As that of a corpse, finger-nails grown immeasureably long,
As they do in the grave, little white eyes, and hardly
Any face at all?
Cold lightning-like, unpleasant, light and blue
Like having one's cold spots intoxicated with mescal!
Looking down a street the houses seemed
Long pointed teeth like a ferret's over the slit
Of a crooked unspeakable smile (like the Thracian woman's
When Thales fell in the well); and the smell reminded me
Of the odeur de souris of Balzac's Cousin Pons
Or Yankee advts about Halitosis and underarm odour.
All the strength seemed to leave my body as I looked.
It sucked the blood from my brain and heart like a vampire,
A hag whose soul-gelding ugliness would chill
To eternal chastity a cantharidized satyr,
And a deadly grey weariness fell over my thoughts like dust.
A terrible shadow descended like dust over my thoughts,
Almost like reading a *Glasgow Herald* leader
Or any of our Scottish local papers,
Smug class organs, standardized, superficial,
Unfair in the presentation of news, and worse than useless
As interpreters of the present scene or guides to the future,
Or like the dread darknesses that descend on one
Who, as the result of an accident sustained
In the course of his favourite recreation, tricycling,
Suffers every now and then from loss of memory.

Whenever the faintest promise, the slightest integrity,
Dares to show in any of the arts or thought or politics,
At once the jealous senile jabber breaks out,
Striking with sure instinct at everything with courage and sincerity.
"Confound it all! If once we let these young folk in
What is to become of us?" A cat on a hot brick
Is a study in repose compared to them
When any new talent's about. — Haydn of Beethoven,
Grétry of Mozart, Handel of Gluck, Rossini of Weber,
Out-Haydn'd, out-Grétry'd, out-Handel'd, out Rossini'd
By mannikins a million times pettier still
Than any of these were to their hated betters!

Blocked out by Robertons and Rosslyn Mitchells,
By Hetheringtons and all the hopeless Hope Street rabble,
Scott[3] and myself! — Who knows in this infernal broth-like fog
There may be greater artists yet by far than we
Unheard of, even by us, condemned to be invisible
In this Tarnhelm of unconscionable ignorance,
Where "everybody is entitled to his own opinion"?

All classes in the city are alike in this,
Running the whole gamut of life from A to B,
University professors, school-teachers, journalists,
Ministers, and all that awful gang of mammalia,
The high mucky-mucks! Bogged in servile and illiberal studies
They have all the same pettifogging spirit,
So narrow it shows little but its limits,
The same incapacity for culture and creative work,
(Glasgow, *arida nutrix* of hundreds of thousands of callous Scots,
Incapable of any process of spiritual growth and conquest,
Destitute of all rich and lively experience,
Without responsibility or honour,
Completely insensitive to any of the qualities
That make for a life worth having,
Pusillanimous and frigid time-servers,

Cold with a *pietrosita* deeper than the masonry accounts for
Though that would satisfy a theorist *à la Taine!*)
As the shopkeepers and the street-corner keelies.
(And constantly in the eyes of these keelies
We see an experience which contains a criticism of modern existence
That cannot be parried by observing that after all
These keelies are cowardly, untrustworthy, and lascivious
Since we cannot declare our most prominent citizens
Less monstrous and inhuman,
Or any razor-slasher different in kind
From a bold knight of old or modern V.C.
"Then they should be all in the army" — learning like beasts
To make movements when they hear a shout!)
The only difference is they have some patter-off, class shibboleths
— But Berlioz, Wagner, Heine, Nietzsche, Orage,
Beethoven, Mozart, Gluck, Weber — it is hell
To think of men of such stature in Glasgow,
To think of any man at all that is more than a louse!

Hugh MacDiarmid, 1947

---

[1] *Blind art thou in thine ears, in thy mind, and in thine eyes.*
Sophocles, Oedipus Rex, 371
[2] *Is it possible that all realities are nothing to them, that their life
runs on, unconnected with anything, like a watch in an empty
room.*
Rainer Maria Rilke
[3] **Francis George Scott,** the composer

NIGHT PILLION

Eleven struck. The traffic lights were green.
The shuddering machine let out its roar
As we sprang forward into brilliant streets.
Beyond your shoulders and helmet the walls rose
Well into darkness, mounted up, plunged past —
Hunting the clouds that hunted the few stars.
And now the neons thinned, the moon was huge.
The gloomy river lay in a glory, the bridge
In its mists as we rode over it slowly sighed,
We lost the shining tram-lines in the slums
As we kept south; the shining trolley-wires
Glinted through Gorbals; on your helmet a glint hung.
A cat in a crumbling close-mouth, a lighted window
With its shadow-play, a newspaper in the wind —
The night swept them up even as we slowed,
Our wheels jolting over the buckled causeys.
But my net swept up night and cat and road
And mine is the shadow-play that window showed
And mine the paper with its cries and creases.
— Shadow-play? What we flashed past was life
As what we flash into is life, and life
Will not stand still until within one flash
Of words or paint or human love it stops
Transfixed, and drops its pain and grime
Into forgetful time.
But I remember: I saw the flash: and then
We met the moonlit Clyde again, swung off
And roared in a straight run for Rutherglen.
The wind whistled by the football ground
And by the waste ground that the seagulls found.
The long wail of a train recalled the city
We had left behind, and mingled with the wind.
Whatever it was that sang in me there
As we neared home, I give it no name here.

But tenements and lives, the wind, our wheels,
The vibrant windshield and your guiding hands
Fell into meaning, whatever meaning it was —
Whatever joy it was —
And my blood quickened in me as I saw
Everything guided, vibrant, where our shadow
Glided along the pavements and the walls.
Perhaps I only saw the thoroughfares,
The river, the dancing of the foundry-flares?
Joy is where long solitude dissolves.
I rode with you towards human needs and cares.

Edwin Morgan, 1957

RAIN IN SAUCHIEHALL STREET

Dowie the air,
Darker nor dayligaun at heich-o-day,
A soss o smeik whaur licht and colour dee,
A blash o blinteran rain whaur lauchters smore.

Dowie the lift,
Baudrons wi belly laich and draigled fur
Creep-creepan owre the sclates, a crawl o fear
That looks to faa but somewey bides alaft.

Dowie the street,
Stanie siver fyled by soot and glaur
Whas blackened waas in scaurs o shadow lour
On barkit kerbs and causeys, thrang wi threat.

Dowie the croud,
Buttoned coats to haud the rain awa
And faces buttoned ticht fornent their wae —
"Better they grat their grief," the makar cried.

Alexander Scott, 1959

The Deluge. Brush and ink, c.1950. Bet Low

Sleet, Gorbals, 1968. Oscar Marzaroli

43

GLASGOW BEASTS,

An a Burd haw, an Inseks, an, aw, a Fush

(Tae Shimpei Kusano)

see me
wan time
ah wis a fox
an wis ah sleekit! ah
gaed slinkin
       heh
an snappin
       yeh
the blokes
aa sayed ah wis a GREAT fox
aw nae kiddin
ah wis pretty good
had a whole damn wood
in them days
hen

An wan time
ah wis a moose
a richt wee douce
chap
Maw
kep sayin
haw
hint
it
awful
an
it's
aa
a
trap

chums
this time
ah wis a bed-bug
Dostoevsky
yelly caurs
cawd
Haw Desire
an
here wee me

an wance
ah wis a zebra
heh heh
crossin

anither
time
ah wis a
minnie
aw
the pond
haw
the shoogly caur
gaun
see s
a frond
fir
ma wee jaur

syne
ah wis a midgie
neist a stank
foon that kin o
thankless
didjye
ever
spen
a
hail simmer
stottin
up
an
doon

45

Hooch
a heilan coo
wis mair liker
it
   the hiker
s
hoo hoos
ferr feart
o ma
herr-do

an wance
ah wis a budgie
   like
Wee Davie
123
Garscadden Road
(oot Polmadie)

honess
pals
like
no been born
a cleg
s e bess

ho
it wis a laugh
been
a giraffe like
ma neck
goat sneckit
in this tree
so ah says
haw Sara
an she says whit
way ur ye staunin
aa bandy-leggit?
bandy-leggit
ah says
so help me
get
yir
giraffe
free

come back
as a coal-hoarse
ho the
       heavy
an
hauf the day
wi yir piece
hauf-etten
hung
roon yir
ear

Ian Hamilton Finlay, 1961

"Hard-up". Brush and ink, c.1950. Bet Low

48   Street life, Crosshill, 1976. George Oliver

COD LIVER OIL AND ORANGE JUICE

It was oot o the east there came a hard man
Aw haw, aa the wey fae Brigton
Chorus:
> *Ah-ha, Glory Hallelujah,*
> *The cod liver oil and the orange juice.*

He went intae a pub and he came oot paraletic,
Ah haw, the VP and the cider.

Does this bus go tae the Denny-Palais,
Aw haw, Ah'm lookin fur a lumber.

In the Palais he met Hairy Mary
Aw haw, the floer o the Calton.

He says tae her, Tell me hen are ye dancin?
Aw naw, it's jist the wey Ah'm staunin.

He says tae her, You're wan in a million.
Aw haw, so's your chances.

Can Ah run ye hame Ah've goat a pair o sannies
Aw haw, you're helluva funny.

Up the back close and doon the dunny
Aw naw, it wisnae fur the first time.

Her maw came oot tae go tae the didgy
Aw haw, he buggered off sharpish.

She tried tae find the hard man, he's jined the Foreign Legion
Aw haw, Sahara and the camels.

So Hairy Mary had a little baby,
Aw haw, its faither's in the army.

Carl MacDougall, 1962

TO JOAN EARDLEY

Pale yellow letters
humbly straggling across
the once brilliant red
of a broken shop-face
CONFECTIO
and a blur of children
at their games, passing,
gazing as they pass
at the blur of sweets
in the dingy, cosy
Rottenrow window —
an Eardley on my wall.
Such rags and streaks
that master us! —
that fix what the pick
and bulldozer have crumbled
to a dingier dust,
the living blur
fiercely guarding
energy that has vanished,
cries filling still
the unechoing close!
I wandered by the rubble
and the houses left standing
kept a chill, dying life
in their islands of stone.
No window opened
as the coal cart rolled
and the coalman's call
fell coldly to the ground.
But the shrill children
jump on my wall.

Edwin Morgan, 1962

THE STARLINGS IN GEORGE SQUARE

I

Sundown on the high stonefields!
The darkening roofscape stirs —
thick — alive with starlings
gathered singing in the square —
like a shower of arrows they cross
the flash of a western window,
they bead the wires with jet,
they nestle preening by the lamps
and shine, sidling by the lamps
and sing, shining, they stir
the homeward hurrying crowds.
A man looks up and points
smiling to his son beside him
wide-eyed at the clamour on those cliffs —
it sinks, shrills out in waves,
levels to a happy murmur,
scatters in swooping arcs,
a stab of confused sweetness
that pierces the boy like a story,
a story more than a song.
He will never forget that evening,
the silhouette of the roofs,
the starlings by the lamps.

II

The City Chambers are hopping mad.
Councillors with rubber plugs in their ears!
Secretaries closing windows!
Window-cleaners want protection and danger money.
The Lord Provost can't hear herself think, man.
What's that?
Lord Provost, can't hear herself think.

At the General Post Office
the clerks write Three Pounds Starling in the savings-books.
Each telephone-booth is like an aviary.
I tried to send a parcel to County Kerry but —
The cables to Cairo got fankled, sir.
What's that?
I said the cables to Cairo got fankled.

And as for the City Information Bureau —
I'm sorry I can't quite chirrup did you twit —
No I wanted to twee but perhaps you can't cheep —
Would you try once again, that's better, I — sweet —
When's the last boat to Milngavie? Tweet?
What's that?
I said when's the last boat to Milngavie?

III

There is nothing for it now but scaffolding:
clamp it together, send for the bird-men,
Scarecrow Strip for the window-ledge landings,
Cameron's Repellent on the overhead wires.
Armour our pediments against eavesdroppers.
This is a human outpost. Save our statues.
Send back the jungle. And think of the joke:
as it says in the papers, It is very comical
to watch them alight on the plastic rollers
and take a tumble. So it doesn't kill them?
All right, so who's complaining? This isn't Peking
where they shoot the sparrows for hygiene and cash.
So we're all humanitarians, locked in our cliff-dwellings
encased in our repellent, guano-free and guilt-free.
The Lord Provost sings in her marble hacienda.
The Postmaster-General licks an audible stamp.
Sir Walter is vexed that his column's deserted.
I wonder if we really deserve starlings?

There is something to be said for these joyous messengers
that we repel in our indignant orderliness.
They lift up the eyes, they lighten the heart,
and some day we'll decipher that sweet frenzied whistling
as they wheel and settle along our hard roofs
and take those grey buttresses for home.
One thing we know they say, after their fashion.
They like the warm cliffs of man.

Edwin Morgan, 1962

George Square: First World War Memorial and City Chambers, c.1965.
Oscar Marzaroli

KING BILLY

Grey over Riddrie the clouds piled up,
dragged their rain through the cemetery trees.
The gates shone cold. Wind rose
flaring the hissing leaves, the branches
swung, heavy, across the lamps.
Gravestones huddled in drizzling shadow,
flickering streetlight scanned the requiescats,
a name and an urn, a date, a dove
picked out, lost, half regained.
What is this dripping wreath, blown from its grave
red, white, blue, and gold
'To Our Leader of Thirty years Ago' —

Bareheaded, in dark suits, with flutes
and drums, they brought him here, in procession
seriously, King Billy of Brigton, dead,
from Bridgeton Cross: a memory of violence,
brooding days of empty bellies,
billiard smoke and a sour pint,
boots or fists, famous sherrickings,
the word, the scuffle, the flash, the shout,
bloody crumpling in the close,
bricks for papish windows, get
the Conks next time, the Conks ambush
the Billy Boys, the Billy Boys the Conks till
Sillitoe scuffs the razors down the stank —
No, but it isn't the violence they remember
but the legend of a violent man
born poor, gang-leader in the bad times
of idleness and boredom, lost in better days,
a bouncer in a betting club,
a quiet man at last, dying
alone in Bridgeton in a box bed.
So a thousand people stopped the traffic

for the hearse of a folk hero and the flutes
threw 'Onward Christian Soldiers' to the winds
from unironic lips, the mourners kept
in step, and there were some who wept.

Go from the grave. The shrill flutes
are silent, the march dispersed.
Deplore what is to be deplored,
and then find out the rest.

Edwin Morgan, 1963

GLASGOW GREEN

Clammy midnight, moonless mist.
A cigarette glows and fades on a cough.
Meth-men mutter on benches,
pawed by river fog. Monteith Row
sweats coldly, crumbles, dies
slowly. All shadows are alive.
Somewhere a shout's forced out — 'No!' —
it leads to nothing but silence,
except the whisper of the grass
and the other whispers that fill the shadows.

'What d'ye mean see me again?
D'ye think I came here jist for that?
I'm no finished with you yet.
I can get the boys t'ye, they're no that faur away.
You wouldny like that eh? Look there's no two ways aboot it.
Christ but I'm gaun to have you Mac
if it takes all night, turn over you bastard
turn over, I'll ——'
                    Cut the scene.

Here there's no crying for help,
it must be acted out, again, again.
This is not the delicate nightmare
you carry to the point of fear
and wake from, it is life, the sweat
is real, the wrestling under a brush
is real, the dirty starless river
is the real Clyde, with a dishrag dawn
it rinses the horrors of the night
but cannot make them clean,
though washing blows

                 where the women watch
by day,
      and children run,
                 on Glasgow Green.

And how shall these men live?
Providence, watch them go!
Watch them love, and watch them die!
How shall the race be served?
It shall be served by anguish
as well as by children at play.
It shall be served by loneliness
as well as by family love.
It shall be served by hunter and hunted in their endless chain
as well as by those who turn back the sheets in peace.
The thorn in the flesh!
Providence, water it!
Do you think it is not watered?
Do you think it is not planted?
Do you think there is not a seed of the thorn
as there is also a harvest of the thorn?
Man, take in that harvest!
Help that tree to bear its fruit!
Water the wilderness, walk there, reclaim it!
Reclaim, regain, renew! Fill the barns and the vats!

Longing,
     longing
          shall find its wine.

Let the women sit in the Green
and rock their prams as the sheets
blow and whip in the sunlight.
But the beds of married love
are islands in a sea of desire.
Its waves break here, in this park,
splashing the flesh as it trembles
like driftwood through the dark.

Edwin Morgan, 1963

Washing on Glasgow Green (Templetons in the background), 1947. George Oliver

TRIO

Coming up Buchanan Street, quickly, on a sharp winter evening
a young man and two girls, under the Christmas lights —
The young man carries a new guitar in his arms,
the girl on the inside carries a very young baby,
and the girl on the outside carries a chihuahua.
And the three of them are laughing, their breath rises
in a cloud of happiness, and as they pass
the boy says, 'Wait till he sees this but!'
The chihuahua has a tiny Royal Stewart tartan coat like a teapot-
    holder,
the baby in its white shawl is all bright eyes and mouth like favours
    in a fresh sweet cake,
the guitar swells out under its milky plastic cover, tied at the neck
    with silver tinsel tape and a brisk sprig of mistletoe.
Orphean sprig! Melting baby! Warm chihuahua!
The vale of tears is powerless before you.
Whether Christ is born, or is not born, you
put paid to fate, it abdicates
                                under the Christmas lights.
Monsters of the year
go blank, are scattered back,
can't bear this march of three.

— And the three have passed, vanished in the crowd
(yet not vanished, for in their arms they wind
the life of men and beasts, and music,
laughter ringing them round like a guard)
at the end of this winter's day.

Edwin Morgan, 1963

THE GLASGOW UNDERGROUND

I know a lot of folk go fancy places at the Fair
They like to sail on steamers or to hurtle through the air
But I've a favourite route that goes to many ports of call
Although unless you looked you'd never notice it at all

Chorus:
There's Partick Cross and Cessnock,
Hillheid and Merkland Street
George's Cross and Govan Cross
Where a' the people meet
West Street, Shields Road
The train goes round and round
Oh it's lovely going your holidays
On the Glasgow Underground.

Clifford Hanley, 1963

Last days of the Glasgow Underground, 1977. Oscar Marzaroli

"glasgow's full of artists"

glasgow's full of artists
they're three feet tall
and eat sherbet dabs

Alan Jackson, 1965

GLASGOW NIGHT

In the world there is fog
         and rain
         and mud
         and grease
         and stench
that's the cargo that Glasgow
unloads on my mind
and this night it's all there:
         the fog
         the rain
         the mud
         the grease
         the stench
while I improvise a lonely blues
to which the boats contribute
boat that comes up the river
boat that goes down the river
fog-horns in action
the one sounding: glas
the other: gow
as though the city
were blowing trombone
ready to jazz with the sea

60

Kenneth White, 1966

"Golden-haired lass", Gorbals, 1964. Oscar Marzaroli

THIS IS MY STORY

This is my city.
My home.
My ain biggin.

Big town,
Boom town,
Brawling town —

but suddenly beautiful,
if you are alive to sudden beauty.

Not the artifice of the town planner,
nor the set piece poised on its pedestal.

An anarchy of sky line,
domed and turreted,
heaving and falling.

Victorian as a covered table leg.

Not to be sold to strangers
by a slogan,
'No mean city',
'Second of the Empire',
'Dear Green Place'.

This city is the story of my life.

Not to be reduced to formulae
but to be learned — by heart.

Not to be trapped
by the wide loop of statistics.

University Tower, with statue of Lord
Roberts, 1970. O.M.

Two Universities —
one medieval;
six theatres;
Colleges of art and music,
drama and domestic science;
Births, marriages, and deaths,
crime rates and convictions.

God knows how many spires
point up to Him.

Provosts have painted it
without a blemish;
Tuppence coloured supplements
have drawn a wart
and sold it as a map.

In season,
weather permitting,
its spiritual cripples go,
singing,
to Paradise or Ibrox.

C.R. Mackintosh: Glasgow School
of Art, c.1930. Annan

Sick with self-love
These images of bandy-legged gods
fused to a many-headed monster
vomit abuse
and the occasional missile.

This is my city.

A Billy or a Dan
or an old tin can.

Hail Glasgow, stern and wild,
fit nurse for an aggressive child!
Old men whose blood is tamed by time
shake scarred grey heads at young men's crime,
and men whose blood was always tame
think every man was born the same,
seek answers in a scientific fog,
and hold that man's less culpable than dog.

John Knox overlooking the
Necropolis, 1964, O.M.

My home.
My ain biggin.

Not a pageant of the past.
It ploughs its history under council houses,
tucks it in corners — and forgets.

But it is old as any town.

Clippers have brought the East
into its docks.
Typhoid, and plague, and cholera
have walked its wynds
and vennels.
Riot has stormed its streets
and the industrial degradation
grimed its walls.

The wind that shook a King down
blew from here —
and here a Queen was overthrown,

Glasgow from Royston Road, c.1962. O.M.

63

but kings and queens crawl
under the belly of its history of making.

Ships are made here.
Slide down its slipways
to the coffee-coloured Clyde
and sail out —
flanked by cranes that rear
like rampant monsters —
to the sea.

Ironworks burn, like sordid hells
in which damnation has no grandeur.

Shipbuilding at John Brown's, 1962. O.M.

Flame, smoke, and sweat
have forged this city
on a hard anvil.

Irish and Scottish bloods
clash and commingle in its veins,
its anarchy,
and in its sentimental,
bloody-minded Friday voice.

Water, and coal, and iron
made this city great;
carried its name,
its fame,
its accent,
to each corner of the world
that's bound and separated by the sea.

It is a giving town.
Weather permitting,
its heart is warm.
There are no strangers in its gates,
but in some corners,
like a fog that will not lift
nor be dispelled,

depression hangs.

Orange March (Maxwell Street), 1964. O.M.

Skinnymalinky long-legs
umbrella feet,
sits in the spittle-smitten street,
Hunch-cuddy hunkered
on gully legs,
the bottle dwindled to its dregs.

Ring-a-ring-a-roses
a pocketful of posies,
Penny buff and the bottle full.
The cat-green, cabbage-green
smelling closes
spewed them out to the ragged school.

Children in derelict back court, 1961. O.M.

Huntygowk, free-the-bed,
tig and peever
Bandy-legs and scabby head.
Ringworm, rickets
and scarlet fever,
Joe loves Mary, Jean loves Fred.

When the drum-tap beats
your pulse to willing,
Shake off the building's coat of black.
Put on your glory for a shilling,
the armistice will take it back.

Join the corner congregations,
pick up dog ends, booze and bum.
The pitch and toss is your salvation;
the pools your hope for years to come.

Skinnymalinky long-legs
umbrella feet
sits in the spittle-smitten street,
Hunch-cuddy hunkered
on gully legs,
the bottle dwindled to its dregs.

Its history is of life, not of events.

Sandwich-board men, Queen Street,
1974. G.O.

65

In season,
weather permitting,
starlings, like squeaky grates,
flood its stone canyons
with spine-chilling song,
and drop their benison
upon the place beneath.

Kelvingrove Park, c.1963. O.M.

Weather permitting,
in the parks,
old men feed duck flotillas,
dogs are unleashed,
and tomorrow's citizens —
righteous or delinquent —
do battle,
skin their knees,
and break their hearts for poky hats.

The streets blossom with giggles of girls,
swans lord over the lochs,
blue mountains creep up close
to peer over the tenements,
and the gasometer shines out
like a martian tower.

This is my city
big, brawling, barbarous —
shrugging off my definition.

In season,
neon rainbows arch
across its black glass streets,
eaves drip and buses splash.

Anthologies of pros
cluster the permitted area,
little men in sandshoes
pad the lanes,
and lovers make deserted islands
in shop doors and closes.

Anniesland-Temple Canal, 1972. G.O.

Honey, the night is full of stars;
depots have swallowed up the cars;
the policeman's torch has peered and gone
and darkness hugs where it has shone.
Come down, come down, out of the dark.
The moon makes christmas in the park.

The whisky drinkers and the meths
have gone to find their separate deaths.
Silence has swept behind their feet
the startled stillness of the street.
Come down, come down, though chimney pots
castle your roof, your rone pipe rots.

Regardless of weather,
art is made —
and no one cares.
Painter and poet,
singer and sculptor
work for deaf ears,
blind eyes,
and foreign accolades.
Free from temptation;
from the pander and the philistine;
from culture in its Sunday suit.

Looking towards the Gorbals, 1965. O.M.

Free as a stray dog.

This is my city.
On its iron gates are wrought with pride
the names of the illustrious dead
that it rejected in their lives.

This is my river
flexing and swelling
under its spanning arteries.
Moon-scrabbled,
neon-dyed and dappled,
stabbed by the thrusting lamplight.

River Clyde and bridges, 1982. G.O.

This is my soaring skeleton
of steel.

This is my body broken unto you.

After the successful operation
will the patient die?
Or will the big barbarian
be born again all straight lines
and sterility.

How, in humanity, can I regret
the amputation of a cankered limb?
How miss the shoogly tram cars?
Townhead? — Gorbals?
How hate the egg-boxes
that have replaced
the hated, loved, and lousy slums?

And yet these scars are mine.

This is my story,
this is my song.
I can no more define it
than define myself.

Tom Wright, 1967

Procession for the last trams in Glasgow, 1962.
Glasgow Herald.

Montrose Street, 1962. O.M.

SIX GLASGOW POEMS

1 The Good Thief

heh jimmy
yawright ih
stull wayiz urryi
ih

heh jimmy
ma right insane yirra pape
ma right insane yirwanny uz jimmy
see it nyir eyes
wanny uz

heh

heh jimmy
lookslik wirgonny miss thi gemm
gonny mis thi GEMM jimmy
nearly three a cloke thinoo

dork init
good jobe they've gote thi lights

2 Simple Simon

thurteen bluddy years wi thim ih
no even a day aff
jiss gee im thi fuckin heave
weeks noatiss nur nuthin
gee im thi heave
thats aw

ahll tellyi sun
see if ah wiz Scot Symon
ahd tell thim wherrty stuff their team
thi hole fuckin lota thim
thats right

a bluddy skandal thats whit it iz
a bluddy skandal

sicken yi

3 Cold, isn't it

wirraw init thigithir missyz
geezyir kross

4 A scream

yi mist yirsell so yi did
we aw skiptwirr ferz njumptaffit thi lights
YIZIR AW PINE THEY FERZ THIMORRA
o it wizza scream
thaht big shite wiz dayniz nut

tellnyi jean
we wirraw shoutn backit im
rrose shoutit shi widny puhllit furra penshin
o yi shooda seeniz face
hi didny no wherrty look

thing iz tay
thirz nay skool thimorra
thi daft kunt wullny even getiz bluddy ferz

5 The miracle of the burd and the fishes

ach sun
jiss keepyir chin up
dizny day gonabootlika hawf shut knife
inaw jiss cozzy a burd

luvur day yi
ach well
gee it a wee while sun
thirz a loat merr fish in thi sea

70

6 Good style

helluva hard tay read theez init
stull
if yi canny unnirston thim jiss clear aff then
gawn
get tay fuck ootma road

ahmaz goodiz thi lota yiz so ah um
ah no whit ahm dayn
tellnyi
jiss try enny a yir fly patir wi me
stick thi bootnyi good style
so ah wull

Tom Leonard, 1967

GLASGOW SABBATH

Rum submerges
rain sheets off the dull heft of the Cuillin
ragged cattle
stand in their dunged pool at Elgol

and south by wet Mull
papercups half-buried in the beach at Dervaig
and the stunned Co-op van
with its tourquoise sans serif motif

to the bubonic snatch of Glasgow
where volatile as monkeys
we die before our time
dazed with morphine in tiled wards

cloudcover sagging
a few stores open selling stale sliced bread
and coarse-faced couples
making for the coast

the streets littered
with hectic old women en route to vote for Christ
two or three late
croupiers and musicians in gaberdine

and a high-stepping paranoiac
agitating his metabolism in the dank park
where laurels drip and pale red
goldfish ruffle the milky mucus on their skins.

Tom Buchan, 1967

THE COMING OF THE WEE MALKIES

Whit'll ye dae when the wee Malkies come,
if they dreep doon affy the wash-hoose dyke,
an pit the hems oan the sterrheid light,
an play wee heidies oan the clean close-wa,
an bloo'er yir windae in wi the baw,
missis, whit'll ye dae?

Whit'll ye dae when the wee Malkies come,
if they chap yir door an choke yir drains,
an caw the feet fae yir sapsy weans,
an tummle thur wulkies through yir sheets,
an tim thur ashes oot in the street,
missis, whit'll ye dae?

Whit'll ye dae when the wee Malkies come,
if they chuck thur screwtaps doon the pan,
an stick the heid oan the sanit'ry man;
when ye hear thum shauchlin doon yir loaby,
chantin, "Wee Malkies! The gemme's a bogey!"
— Haw, missis, whit'll ye dae?

72   **Stephen Mulrine**, 1967

Gorbals back court, 1963. Oscar Marzaroli

Gorbals: looking towards the Sir Basil Spence high-rise blocks during construction, 1964. Oscar Marzaroli

74 Last of the old Gorbals tenements, Hutchesontown, 1968. Oscar Marzaroli

THE JEELY PIECE SONG

I'm a skyscraper wean; I live on the nineteenth flair,
But I'm no' gaun oot tae play ony mair,
'Cause since we moved tae Castlemilk, I'm wastin' away
'Cause I'm gettin' wan meal less every day:

Ch. *Oh ye cannae fling pieces oot a twenty storey flat,*
   Seven hundred hungry weans'll testify to that.
   If it's butter, cheese or jeely, if the breid is plain or pan,
   The odds against it reaching earth are ninety-nine tae wan.

On the first day ma maw flung oot a daud o' Hovis broon;
It came skytin' oot the windae and went up insteid o' doon.
Noo every twenty-seven hoors it comes back intae sight
'Cause ma piece went intae orbit and became a satellite.

On the second day ma maw flung me a piece oot wance again.
It went and hut the pilot in a fast low-flying plane.
He scraped it aff his goggles, shouting through the intercom,
"The Clydeside Reds huv goat me wi' a breid-an-jeely bomb."

On the third day ma maw thought she would try another throw.
The Salvation Army band was staunin' doon below.
"Onward, Christian Soldiers" was the piece they should've played
But the oompah man was playing a piece an' marmalade.

We've wrote away to Oxfam to try an' get some aid,
An' a' the weans in Castlemilk have formed a "piece brigade."
We're gonnae march to George's Square demanding civil rights
Like nae mair hooses ower piece-flinging height.

Adam McNaughtan, 1967

GLASGOW NOCTURNE

Materialised from the flaked stones of buildings
dank with neglect and poverty the pack,
thick-shouldered, slunk through rows of offices
squirting anonymous walls with their own lack

of self-identity. Tongs ya bass, Fleet,
Fuck the Pope spurted like blood: a smear
protesting to the passing daylight folk
the prowled-up edge of menace, the spoor of fear

that many waters cannot quench, or wash
clean from what hands, what eyes, from what hurt hearts?
O Lord! the preacher posed at the park gates,
what must we do to be whole in all our parts?

Late on Saturday night, when shop fronts doused
their furniture, contraceptives, clothes and shoes,
violence sneaked out in banded courage,
bored with hopelessness that has nothing to lose.

A side-street shadow eyed two lovers together;
he, lured from the loyalties of the gang
by a waif who wore her sex like a cheap trinket;
she, touched to her woman's need by his wrong

tenderness. On the way from their first dance,
the taste of not enough fumbled their search
of hands and lips endeared in a derelict close.
Over the flarepath of their love, a lurch

thrust from the shadow, circling their twined bodies.
It left them clung before its narrowing threat
till she shrieked. They peeled her from her lover,
a crumpled sob of a doll dropped in the street,

while he received his lesson: ribs and jaw
broken, kidneys and testicles ruptured, a slit

where the knife licked his groin. Before he died
in the ambulance, she'd vanished. Shops lit

up their furniture, contraceptives, clothes and shoes
again. Next morning, there was a darker stain
than Tongs ya bass and Fleet on the edge of the kerb;
but it disappeared in the afternoon rain.

Maurice Lindsay, 1968

the docks on Sunday

      Hulks, ruined warehouses
echo the blasting radio from the hammer-tin
place across the estuary
The grasses blow, send their purple and white
crestfeathers floating
      Sunny SUNDAY
      Water moving, and I too
in imagined movement
      THINGS
      cold and bitter smell
of roasted iron and squashed boxes
      rusty tins, bed springs
shadow on the mulchy peat
      NOISE
      seagull cry.
The two walk on the dirty shore, crunch.

Blue trains run, clatters and squealing
　　　bus brakes
CRACKING corrugated tin SHATTERING
foottrodden glass
　　　　　　waste dockland
Bagpipes shriek past the ricket remains of
wooden watchtowers, deserted tunnel domes
where glass was punched out and flowers float
out . . . out . . . out . . . out . . .

Jean Milton, 1969

　Harland and Wolff site at Govan after clearance, 1964. Oscar Marzaroli

RIDER

i

a grampus whacked the hydrophone / Loch Fyne left its green bed,
  fled / shrieking to Cowal / it all began

the nutcracker closed round Port Glasgow / it snapped with a burst
  of docks and / capstans downwind like collarstuds

cabbage whites in deadlock / were hanged from geans and rowans /
  wedlock-red

Greenock in steam / hammered albatrosses onto packingcases / without
  forgiveness / zam

by the waters of Glasgow / angels hung pilgrims, primroses, Dante,
  black blankets / over and over / the acid streams

a giant hedgehog lifting the Necropolis / solid silver / to the moon /
  sang of the deluge

long keys of gas unlocked the shaking Campsies at / last, at least /
  four drumlins were heard howling / as far as Fenwick Moor

Calderpark was sucked into a belljar, came out / at Kalgoorlie with
  elephants and northern lights

ravening taxis roasted dogs in basements, basted / chicken wheels in
  demolition oil / slept by the swing / of the wrecker's ball

the Holy Loch turned to granite chips, the ships / died with their
  stiff upper lips reaching to Aviemore

Para Handy sculled through the subway with the Stone of Destiny /
  shot the rapids at Cessnock right into Sunday morning

a coelacanth on stilts was setting fire to Sauchiehall Street when Tom
  Leonard /

sold James B.V. Thomson a horse, black /

in the night and dust / which galloped him away /

deep as the grave / writing

ii

Davidson looked through the telescope at MacDiarmid and said / what,
  is that God
                                                               79

Davidson rode off on a blood-splashed stag / into the sea / horses
  ultimately
Davidson sold / fish to Neptune, fire / to Prometheus, to himself /
  a prisoner's iron bed, the red
sun rose flapping slowly over Nietzsche / bars melted into sand /
  black marias stalled in Calton
the rainbow dropped its pot of lead on Peterhead / the peter keys
  were blown to breadcrumbs, fed
to men forbid / the men bought lead, built jails, went mad, lay dead /
  in iron fields
the jaws of Nero smouldered in a dustbin / cinders tingled / the dead
  rose / tamam
sulphur shoes dancing to Mars / their zircon eyeshades flashed,
  beryllium / toeguards clipped Mercury's boulders
Lucretius was found lying under the flary walls / of a universe in the
  Crab nebula / crying
the dancers brought him water / where he lay he rose, froze / in a
  mandala like a flame / blessing
the darkness of all disbelievers / filaments of the Crab wrapped him
  in hydrogen shroud / remade
he walked by Barrhead and Vauxhall Bridge, by the sea waited / with
  his dark horse in the dangerous night air
for a rider / his testament
delivered to the earth, kicking /
the roots of things

iii

five hundred million hummingbirds sat in the Kelvin Hall / three
  hundred thousand girls took double basses
in a crocodile to Inverkip / six thousand children drew Rothesay
  through twelve thousand kites / two hundred
plumbers with morning cellos galvanized the bedmakers of Fairlie /
  forty babies
threw their teething-rings at a helicopter / trickety-track / till
80   Orpheus looked back

and there was nothing but the lonely hills and sky unless the chilling
  wind was something / and the space
of pure white pain where his wife had held his hand from hell / he
  left the place
and came to a broken shack at midday / with carts and horses /
  strong dark ragged boys
played in the smoke / the gypsies gave him soup and bread / for the
  divine brooch / who cares
what is divine, he said / and passed into the valley of the Clyde,
  a cloud / followed
and many campfires in that landscape, dogs whining, cuckoos,
  glasshouses, thundershowers /
David Gray shook the rain from his hair and held his heart, the
  Luggie flashed
in the lightning of the last March storm / he led a sweet brown mare
  into the mist / the apple-boughs
closed over, where the flute
of Orpheus was only wished for /
in the drip of trees

iv

butcher-boys tried to ward off sharks / the waters rose quickly /
  great drowned bankers
floated from bay-windows / two housemaids struggled on Grosvenor
  Terrace with a giant conger
the Broomielaw was awash with slime and torn-out claws and
  anchor-flakes / rust and dust
sifted together where a dredger ploughed up the Gallowgate / pushed a
  dirty wave over Shettleston
spinning shopfronts crashed in silence / glassily, massively /
  porticoes tilting / settled in mud
lampreys fastened on four dead sailors drifting through Finnieston /
  in a Drygate attic
James Macfarlan threw his pen at the stinking wall / the whisky and
  the stinking poverty

ran down like ink / the well of rats was bottomless and Scotch / the
  conman and the conned
fought on / the ballads yellowed, the pubs filled / at Anderston he
  reached his grave in snow / selah
the ruined cities were switched off / there was no flood / his father
  led a pedlar's horse
by Carrick fields, his mother sang / the boy rode on a jogging back /
  far back / in rags /
Dixon's Blazes roared and threw more poets in its molten pools /
  forges on fire
matched the pitiless bread, the head
long hangdog, the lifted elbow /
the true bloody pathos and sublime

v

Kossuth took a coalblack horse from Debrecen / clattered up
  Candleriggs into the City Hall
three thousand cheers could never drown the groaning fortress-
  bars / a thousand years
heard the wind howl / scimitars, eagles, bugles, edicts, whips,
  crowns, in the pipes / playing / the grave plain in the sun
handcuffed keelies shouted in Albion Street / slogans in red
  fragments broke the cobblestones, Kossuth
drew a mirage on electric air / the hare sat calmly on the
  doorstep / it was Monday over all the world / om
Tom McGrath mixed bread and milk for the young hare / Monk and
  Parker spoke in a corner / the still room
was taken / Dougal Graham stood on his hands, the bell / rang
  between his feet / he rolled
on his hump through the swarming Tontine piazzas, swam / in dogs,
  parcels, puddles, tobacco-quids
ran with a bawbee ballad five feet long / felt fishwives / gutted
  a brace of Glasgow magistrates / lay
with a pig in his arms and cried the city fathers bitches / till
82 a long shadow fell on pedlars

and far away the sound of hoofs / increased in moonlight / whole
  cities crouched in saddlebags
churches, dungeons, juntas dangled from reins / like grasses
  picked from the rank fields
and drops of halter sweat
burned men to the bone, but the hare
like mad / played

Edwin Morgan, 1969

GLASGOW

City, cauldron of a shapeless fire,
bubbling with brash Irish and a future

that stares from fifteen stories towards the Clyde.
The cotton and tobacco plants have died

Plantation St. is withered. You love your ships,
hate your police, in whisky-coloured sleeps

adore your footballers. Victoria's not amused
at Celtic Park or Ibrox where the horsed

dice-capped policeman, seared by pure flame
trot in white gauntlets round your serious game

and the roaring furnaces bank your last pride.
They shed the rotting tenements flying goalward.

Iain Crichton Smith, 1969   83

IN GLASGOW

In my smoochy corner
take me on a cloud
I'll wrap you round
and lay you down
in smoky tinfoil
rings and records
sheets of whisky
and the moon all right
old pal all right
the moon all night

Mercy for the rainy
tyres and the violet
thunder that bring you
shambling and shy
from chains of Easterhouse
plains of lights
make your delight
in my nest my spell
my arms and my shell
my barn my bell

I've combed your hair
and washed your feet
and made you turn
like a dark eel
in my white bed
till morning lights
a silent cigarette
throw on your shirt
I lie staring yet
forget forget

Edwin Morgan, 1970

84

Graffiti, Maryhill, 1980. Ken MacGregor

Easterhouse, 1983. George Oliver

85

NOSTALGIE

Well, the George Squerr stchumers've pit the hems
oan Toonheid's answer tae London's Thames;
thuv peyed a squaad ooty Springburn broo
tae kinfront the Kinawl wi its Watterloo,
an dampt up Monklan's purlin stream
fur some dampt bailie's petrol dream,
some Tory nutter wi caurs oan the brain —
jis shows ye, canny leave nuthin alane,
the scunners.

Aye, thuv waistit Toonheid's claim tae fame,
an minny's the terrs Ah hud as a wean,
fishin fur roach aff the slevvery wa,
an pullin in luckies, mibbe a baw,
ur a bike, even, howked up ooty the glaur —
bit thuv timmed oot the watter, fur chuckies an taur,
jis cowped the Kinawl fulla slag, ten a penny,
an wheecht aw the luckies away tae the Clenny,
in hunners.

An thuv plankt the deid dugs aw swelt wi disease,
an pickt oot thur graves wi wee wizzent trees
tae relieve the monotony, eight tae a mile —
brek wan stick aff, thull gie ye the jile.
Ach, thurs nuthin tae beat a gude pie in the sky,
bit Ah've seen the Kinawl easy-oasyin by,
an it isnae the same Toonheid noo at aw,
an therrs even the rats is shootin the craw —
nae wunners.

Fur thuv drapped an Emm Wan oan the aul Toonheid,
an thurs nae merr dugs gonny float by deid —
jis caurs, jis breezin alang in the breeze,
terrin the leafs aff the hauf-bilet trees,
hell-bent fur the East, (aye, yir no faur wrang)

wi thur taur an thur chuckies tae see thum alang —
ach, nivver mind, son, they kin aw go tae hell,
an we'll jis stick like the Monklan itsel —
non-runners.

Stephen Mulrine, 1971

Townhead, 1974. George Oliver

OBITUARY

We two in W.2
walking,
and all the W.2. ladies, their
hair coiffed and corrugated come
with well-done faces
from the hairdressers.
We together
laughing,
in our snobbery of lovers,
at their narrow vowels
and strange permed poodles.
Locked too long in love, our eyes
were unaccustomed to the commonplace.
        Seems silly now really.

We two in W.2
walking
down Byres Road
passing unconcerned
a whole florist's
full of funerals,
the nightmare butcher's shop's
unnumbered horrors,
the hung fowls
and the cold fish
dead on the slab.
We saw ourselves duplicated
by the dozen in the chainstore
with no crisis of identity.
Headlines on newsagent's placards
caused us no alarm.
Sandwichman's prophecies of doom
just slid off our backs.

The television showroom's window
showed us cities burning
in black and white but we
had no flicker of interest.
An ambulance charged screaming past
but all we noticed was the funny old
Saturday street musician.
        Seems silly now really.

We two one Sunday
at the art galleries
looking only at each other.
We two one Sunday
in the museum —
wondering why the ownership of a famous man
should make a simple object a museum piece —
and I afraid
to tell you how
sometimes I did not wash your coffee cup for days
or touched the books you lent me
when I did not want to read.
Well, even at the time
        that seemed a bit silly really.

Christmas found me
with other fond and foolish girls
at the menswear counters
shopping for the ties that bind.
March found me
guilty of too much hope.
        Seems silly now really.

Liz Lochhead, 1971

CHARING CROSS

digging under —
mining getting
under skin of
city

straight cross sections
cut in houserows
open pan loaf — not yet stale

underneath it all is
soil, basic, real and
food
deep — deep — deeper down

2 men alone in thon
big hole are toys
a wean's left   in a sandpit

an angel wife on the *mitchell*
points accusing down at others
two or three
who fill in time that's left them

they keep on digging, will not find
this city's heart
is superficial, built
on top of not deep under
standing now

they'll tear it down and
digging deeper all the
time

has cut great layers
on this great elephant

held by frost, the
raw flesh hardened
grew definitive and
charing cross had always been

snowed was feminised
and lasting, pliable as
music.

we spent the winter growing
used to area, while gradually
you're putting clothes on
with that look
we'll never see you bare again

and the great wide hunt for
the great black soul of
glasgow wasn't   they
were building
bypass and approach roads
all the time.

Robin Munro, 1971

GLASGOW SONNETS

i

A mean wind wanders through the backcourt trash.
Hackles on puddles rise, old mattresses
puff briefly and subside. Play-fortresses
of brick and bric-a-brac spill out some ash.
Four storeys have no windows left to smash,
but in the fifth a chipped sill buttresses
mother and daughter the last mistresses
of that black block condemned to stand, not crash.
Around them the cracks deepen, the rats crawl.
The kettle whimpers on a crazy hob.
Roses of mould grow from ceiling to wall.
The man lies late since he has lost his job,
smokes on one elbow, letting his coughs fall
thinly into an air too poor to rob.

ii

A shilpit dog fucks grimly by the close.
Late shadows lengthen slowly, slogans fade.
The YY PARTICK TOI grins from its shade
like the last strains of some lost *libera nos
a malo*. No deliverer ever rose
from these stone tombs to get the hell they made
unmade. The same weans never make the grade.
The same grey street sends back the ball it throws.
Under the darkness of a twisted pram
a cat's eyes glitter. Glittering stars press
between the silent chimney-cowls and cram
the higher spaces with their SOS.
Don't shine a torch on the ragwoman's dram.
Coats keep the evil cold out less and less.

91

iii

'See a tenement due for demolition?
I can get ye rooms in it, two, okay?
Seven hundred and nothin legal to pay
for it's no legal, see? That's my proposition,
ye can take it or leave it but. The position
is simple, you want a hoose, I say
for eight hundred pound it's yours.' And they,
trailing five bairns, accepted his omission
of the foul crumbling stairwell, windows wired
not glazed, the damp from the canal, the cooker
without pipes, packs of rats that never tired —
any more than the vandals bored with snooker
who stripped the neighbouring houses, howled, and fired
their aerosols — of squeaking 'Filthy lucre!'

iv

Down by the brickworks you get warm at least.
Surely soup-kitchens have gone out? It's not
the Thirties now. Hugh MacDiarmid forgot
in 'Glasgow 1960' that the feast
of reason and the flow of soul has ceased
to matter to the long unfinished plot
of heating frozen hands. We never got
an abstruse song that charmed the raging beast.
So you have nothing to lose but your chains,
dear Seventies. Dalmarnock, Maryhill,
Blackhill and Govan, better sticks and stanes
should break your banes, for poets' words are ill
to hurt ye. On the wrecker's ball the rains
of greeting cities drop and drink their fill.

v

'Let them eat cake' made no bones about it.
But we say let them eat the hope deferred
and that will sicken them. We have preferred
silent slipways to the riveters' wit.
And don't deny it — that's the ugly bit.
Ministers' tears might well have launched a herd
of bucking tankers if they'd been transferred
from Whitehall to the Clyde. And smiles don't fit
either. 'There'll be no bevvying' said Reid
at the work-in. But all the dignity you muster
can only give you back a mouth to feed
and rent to pay if what you lose in bluster
is no more than win patience with 'I need'
while distant blackboards use you as their duster.

vi

The North Sea oil-strike tilts east Scotland up,
and the great sick Clyde shivers in its bed.
But elegists can't hang themselves on fled-
from trees or poison a recycled cup —
If only a less faint, shaky sunup
glimmered through the skeletal shop and shed
and men washed round the piers like gold and spread
golder in soul than Mitsubishi or Krupp —
The images are ageless but the thing
is now. Without my images the men
ration their cigarettes, their children cling
to broken toys, their women wonder when
the doors will bang on laughter and a wing
over the firth be simply joy again.

vii

Environmentalists, ecologists
and conservationists are fine no doubt.
Pedestrianization will come out
fighting, riverside walks march off the lists,
pigeons and starlings be somnambulists
in far-off suburbs, the sandblaster's grout
multiply pink piebald facades to pout
at sticky-fingered mock-Venetianists.
Prop up's the motto. Splint the dying age.
Never displease the watchers from the grave.
Great when fake architecture was the rage,
but greater still to see what you can save.
The gutted double fake meets the adage:
a wig's the thing to beat both beard and shave.

viii

Meanwhile the flyovers breed loops of light
in curves that would have ravished tragic Toshy —
clean and unpompous, nothing wishy-washy.
Vistas swim out from the bulldozer's bite
by day, and banks of earthbound stars at night
begin. In Madame Emé's Sauchie Haugh, she
could never gain in leaves or larks or sploshy
lanes what's lost in a dead boarded site —
the life that overspill is overkill to.
Less is not more, and garden cities are
the flimsiest oxymoron to distil to.
And who wants to distil? Let bus and car
and hurrying umbrellas keep their skill to
feed ukiyo-e beyond Lochnagar.

ix

It groans and shakes, contracts and grows again.
Its giant broken shoulders shrug off rain.
It digs its pits to a shauchling refrain.
Roadworks and graveyards like their gallus men.
It fattens fires and murders in a pen
and lets them out in flaps and squalls of pain.
It sometimes tears its smoky counterpane
to hoist a bleary fist at nothing, then
at everything, you never know. The west
could still be laid with no one's tears like dust
and barricaded windows be the best
to see from till the shops, the ships, the trust
return like thunder. Give the Clyde the rest.
Man and the sea make cities as they must.

x

From thirtieth floor windows at Red Road
he can see choughs and samphires, dreadful trade —
the schoolboy reading *Lear* has that scene made.
A multi is a sonnet stretched to ode
and some say that's no joke. The gentle load
of souls in clouds, vertiginously stayed
above the windy courts, is probed and weighed.
Each monolith stands patient, ah'd and oh'd.
And stalled lifts generating high-rise blues
can be set loose. But stalled lives never budge.
They linger in the single-ends that use
their spirit to the bone, and when they trudge
from closemouth to laundrette their steady shoes
carry a world that weighs us like a judge.

Edwin Morgan, 1972

BY KELVIN WATER
(For Iain Crichton Smith)

I stood on the bridge
above Kelvin water
(the banks are prohibited)
and saw a piece of muddy ground
for cars to park,
an old man
who hadn't made it
to the subterranean toilet,
dribbling and cursing
in perpetual, mumbled rage,
the children playing
round the backs,
where the rats are,
and on the horizon,
where I expected the prehistoric cranes
of the dead shipyards,
I saw no horizon
but smoke,
and smoke so thick
and permanent
it will outlast the people.

There were trees
and a blackbird, female,
with a white head,
not singing;
from the under-arch of the bridge,
the flash of a wagtail.

In the vaults of the City Chambers
they were perhaps giving approval
to a new skyscraper housing estate
without any people,
or banning another film,
eating a dinner,

working on a plan
for prisoners
to pay rates.

"This life that we love and share."

Below me the river heaved along,
carrying the weight of six days rain,
dead leaves, old tyres, and contraceptives,
splashing up brown, discoloured phlegm
from its poisoned depths.

Tom McGrath, 1972

YOU LIVED IN GLASGOW

You lived in Glasgow many years ago.
I do not find your breath in the air.
It was, I think, in the long-skirted thirties
when idle men stood at every corner
chewing their fag-ends of a failed culture.
Now I sit here in George Square
where the War Memorial's yellow sword glows bright
and the white stone lions mouth at bus and car.
A maxi-skirted girl strolls slowly by.
I turn and look. It might be you. But no.
Around me there's a 1970 sky.

Everywhere there are statues. Stone remains.
The mottled flesh is transient. On those trams,
invisible now but to the mind, you bore
your groceries home to the 1930 slums.
"There was such warmth," you said. The gaslight hums
and large caped shadows tremble on the stair.
Now everything is brighter. Pale ghosts walk
among the spindly chairs, the birchen trees.

In lights of fiercer voltage you are less
visible than when in winter you
walked, a black figure, through the gaslight blue.

The past's an experience that we cannot share.
Flat-capped Glaswegians and the Music Hall.
Apples and oranges on an open stall.
A day in the country. And the sparkling Clyde
splashing its local sewage at the wall.
This April day shakes memories in a shade
opening and shutting like a parasol.
There is no site for the unshifting dead.
You're buried elsewhere though your flickering soul
is a constant tenant of my tenement.

You were happier here than anywhere, you said.
Such fine good neighbours helping when your child
almost died of croup. Those pleasant Wildes
removed with the fallen rubble have now gone
in the building programme which renews each stone.
I stand in a cleaner city, better fed,
in my diced coat, brown hat, my paler hands
leafing a copy of the latest book.
Dear ghosts, I love you, haunting sunlit winds,
dear happy dented ghosts, dear prodigal folk.

I left you, Glasgow, at the age of two
and so you are my birthplace just the same.
Divided city of the green and blue
I look for her in you, my constant aim
to find a ghost within a close who speaks
in Highland Gaelic.
                    The bulldozer breaks
raw bricks to powder. Boyish workmen hang
like sailors in tall rigging. Buildings sail
into the future. The old songs you sang
fade in their pop songs, scale on dizzying scale.

Iain Crichton Smith, 1972

Hutchesontown, 1973. George Oliver

LAMENT FOR A LOST DINNER TICKET

See ma mammy
See ma dinner ticket
A pititnma
Pokit an she pititny
Washnmachine.

See thon burnty
Up wherra firewiz
Ma mammy says Am no tellnyagain
No'y playnit.
A jist wen'y eatma
Pokacrisps furma dinner
Nabigwoffldoon.

The wummin sed Aver near
Clapsd
Jistur heednur
Wee wellies sticknoot.

They sed Wot heppind?
Nme'nma belly
Na bedna hospital.
A sed A pititnma
Pokit an she pititny
Washnmachine.

They sed Ees thees chaild eb slootly
Non verbal?
A sed MA BUMSAIR
Nwen'y sleep.

Margaret Hamilton, 1972

Indian bride, 1982. John Gilmour

SOMETHING I'M NOT

familiar with, the tune
of their talking, comes tumbling before them
down the stairs which (oh I forgot) it was my turn
to do again this week.
My neighbour and my neighbour's child. I nod, we're not
on speaking terms exactly.

I don't know much about her. Her dinners smell
different. Her husband's a busdriver,
so I believe.
She carries home her groceries in Grandfare bags
though I've seen her once or twice around the corner
at Shastri's for spices and such.
(I always shop there — he's open till all hours
making good). How does she feel?
Her children grow up with foreign accents,
swearing in fluent Glaswegian. Her face

101

is sullen. Her coat is drab plaid, hides
but for a hint at the hem, her sari's
gold embroidered gorgeousness. She has
a jewel in her nostril.
The golden hands with the almond nails
that push the pram turn blue
in this city's cold climate.

Liz Lochhead, 1972

GLASGOW GANGS

"Something to do with territory makes them sing."
— **Norman MacCaig,** *Birds All Singing.*

Something to do with territory makes them stab,
The adolescent Apaches,
With nothing to lose but their lives
As they ride the savannahs of exiled slums,
The Castlemilk prairies,
The Easterhouse great plains,
Their hatchets drawn to hack those drab horizons
To sizes and shapes of self,
Themselves to assert
Against against against
All other tribes,
Where each of them makes his manhood
By scalping entire strangers,
While round their fury of renegade fires
The foreigners flood,
The palefaces, white-eyes, powerful generations,
The seventh cavalry always upon command,
The Great White Fathers (living dead)
Whose legislation is lethal,
Killing the exploit, swamping

The mad splendour of *We Are the People*
In deadly dullness, dull deadliness —
Be our Brothers — or Else.

This is their history. Must it repeat
Exactly its criminal errors? Must it expect
The appalling example only? Must it announce
The selfsame judgment over and over and over?

Last time, the Great White Fathers were wicked uncles,
Last time, the braves were blooded
By belting machineguns,
Last time
Was last time.

This time,
Like every time a time of tribulation,
Palefaces offer the pipe of peace,
White-eyes whirl in the ghostdance,
The seventh cavalry rein on a sixth sense.

BUT
                    will the braves believe?

Alexander Scott, 1972

Glasgow graffiti, 1968. Oscar Marzaroli

MONSTER

A monster came out the graveyard down at Caledonia Road
and permeated in story as far as Govanhill.
I almost said, 'clanked', that was my monster.
I saw it as a hellish bone-and-metal thing
teethed with wood, broad-shouldered like Eamonn Andrews.
I didn't believe it but I might have run,
there was a general agreement to. The Record read, CITY KIDS
IN MONSTER PANIC.

     Then soft strangers came
to the school. Was it a massive ape, over the tenements?
Hands up then if it was green and fudgy, enveloping folk
so they processed out the other end as stour and teeth?
That's interesting. The others, did it look like anyone
in your family? (like Auntie Sadie, never washed
her drawers; at my grandma's funeral she started screaming and fighting?
or like Bunton up the stairs, don't go in, he'll give you wine?)
Never in it. I told you it had nothing but teeth,
sharp, and rotten as well. It was seven feet or so,
just big enough to beat a man and sicken him.
But now I suppose we're all grown up, or most of us.

Archie McCallum, 1972

A SENSE OF ORDER

Sunday Walk

I stop at the foot of Garioch Drive
Where my aunt used to live
Three floors up.
          I remember the smell
Of camomile that hit you in the hall,
The embroidered sampler, the jars
Of wax chrysanths, the budgerigars
In their lacquered cage; the ladies who came
To read the Bible in the front room —
Surrounded by marzipan, and dragons
On silky screens.
          A rag-and-bone man,
His pony ready for the knacker's yard,
Rounds a corner (short of a tail-light)
And disappears up Clouston Street.

Below, the Kelvin runs like stinking lard.

Period Piece

Hand in hand, the girls glide
Along Great Western Road.
          Outside
The Silver Slipper the boys wait,
Trousers flared, jacket-pockets
Bulging with carry-outs.
The girls approach. A redhead pouts,
Sticks her tongue out,
Then passes under the strung lights
To the dance-floor. 'I'll have it
Off with that one.' 'Want to bet?'
'I'd rather lumber her mate . . .'

They nick their cigarettes.
          Inside,
The miniskirts are on parade,
Listening to The Marmalade.

Cranworth Street
I climb the tenement stair
With its scoured tiles, its odour
Of cat.
        We lived here, before
My father moved to Ayrshire.
I have not been back, for years.

The brass nameplate, the square
Bellpull, mean nothing any more.
What is there to recapture,
To rediscover? It is too late
In the season, for that.

I cling to the wooden
Rail and, for no reason,
Break out in a sweat
As I reach the street.

Street Scene
The faces outside the Curlers
Explode like fat cigars
In the frosty air.

Even the newspaper-seller
Rocks on his heels, half-seas over.
And I don't blame him.

    As the pictures
Come out, scores of lovers
Head for their parked cars.

Two ladies whisper
Goodnight to each other.
Neither feels secure
Till on her own stair
She snibs the basement door
And breathes freely, behind iron bars.

106   **Stewart Conn, 1972**

FAMILY VISIT

Laying linoleum, my father spends hours
With his tape measure,
Littering the floor
As he checks his figures, gets
The angle right; then cuts
Carefully, to the music
Of a slow logic. In despair
I conjure up a room where
A boy sits and plays with coloured bricks.

My mind tugging at its traces,
I see him in more dapper days
Outside the Kibble Palace
With my grandfather, having
His snapshot taken; men firing
That year's leaves.
The Gardens are only a stone's throw
From where I live . . . But now
A younger self comes clutching at my sleeve.

Botanic Gardens. Etching, 1938. Ian Fleming RSA, RSW

Or off to Innellan, singing, we would go,
Boarding the steamer at the Broomielaw
In broad summer, these boomps-a-daisy
Days, the ship's band playing in a lazy
Swell, my father steering well clear
Of the bar, mother making neat
Packets of waste-paper to carry
To the nearest basket or (more likely)
All the way back to Cranworth Street.

Leaving my father at it
(He'd rather be alone) I take
My mother through the changed Botanics.
The bandstand is gone, and the great
Rain-barrels that used to rot
And overflow. Everything is neat
And plastic. And it is I who must walk
Slowly for her, past the sludge
And pocked marble of Queen Margaret Bridge.

Stewart Conn, 1972

108 Pleasure steamer leaving Bridge Wharf, c.1935. Annan

PARKHEAD CROSS

A miner blue-scarred leashes his whippet
to the railings by the red police-box

On the street skylight over the lavatory
the Close Brethren stand
in a ring round holy ground

A lightning conductor from Heaven
charging the little band with power
a Brother prays

> Let Glasgow flourish
> by the preaching of the Word
> and the praising of Thy name

The prayer dies under steel wheels
loud on tramlines of the double-decker from Tollcross
that stops by the shut greengrocer's

Some leave clutching the brass rod
step up
go inside
climb upstairs
stand on the platform

The tramcar leaves for Glasgow Cross

> Eternity! Eternity!
> Where will you spend eternity?

The singing dies away

William Montgomerie, 1973

SEEN OUT

Over small print in papers,
arguments at Public Inquiries,
a demolition squad moves in;
coloured helmets swarming up to
patched roofs, unpicking rafters,
levering slabs through ceilings,
gulping cupboards sheer with air.
Now and then a tenement
fights back, stumps snarling
chokes of dust, menacing
what once had been a passing street.
Machines bring all stone
down to its own level.

On a half-cleared site where soon
rows of red and yellow curtains
would be switched-on stacks of lights,
I found the handle of a pan,
a mattress spring, a chair's leg,
the bric-a-brac of done-with caring;
while from one grey isolated
tenement storey, with cushions,
blandishments and blankets
they prised loose an old woman
from a sense of place that hadn't
quite seen out her time.

Maurice Lindsay, 1973

110

THE GIRL I MET IN BYRES ROAD

At night I can't remember her, or ever unwounded
With a happy face. We came together too often
With knives in our hands for happiness to
Come out of the struggle.

               I often said
I'd leave her, and she left me, often enough.
We never talked together: long conflicting monologues
Took place between us.

               That was Glasgow
When we were young. You don't have good memories
Of something like that.

               So let me say this
About her: if we went our own ways, and never
Properly parted, it was because we never properly
Met. Two other shadows joined in the darkness
And the shadows that were ourselves remained
Alone.

Robin Hamilton, 1973

"there was that time charlie tully"

there was that time charlie tully
took a corner kick
an' you know how he
wus always great at gettin thaem
tae curve in, well charlie takes the corner
and it curved in and fuck me did the wind
no cerry it right intae the net. but they

Charlie Tully

111

disputed it. and the linesman hud the
flag up and they goat away wae it and tully
hud tae take it again. an' fuck me does he no get
it in the net again. you should've
seen it. it just seemed tae go roon
in a kind o' hauf curcle. above aw their
heids. fuckin' keeper didnae know where tae look.
and there was that time john cassidy went into
the toilet and there was no
lightbulb and he just had to fix up with some
water he found in a bucket. and here it was piss.
he didnae discover it until it was actually in
him. he was very sick after that. he goat
very bad jaundice.

Tom McGrath, 1973

112   Crowd incident, Celtic v Rangers Cup Final at Hampden Park, 1963. Oscar Marzaroli

ARRIVALS

1

The plane meets
its reflection on the wet
runway, then crosses
to where I wait
behind plate glass.

I watch
with a mixture
of longing and despair
as you re-enter
the real world.

All we have is each other.
I sometimes wonder
if that is enough;
whether being together
enlarges or diminishes grief.

2

Remember arriving
from Thorame —
the scent
of honey,
of lavender clinging.

On the Jonte,
climbing goat-tracks
to drink from a spring
under an arch
of red sandstone.

Or last year,
a second honeymoon
in Amsterdam, having
exchanged gifts: a miniature
war-horse, a silver ring.

3

Tonight your return
from Ulster
renders
my fears unfounded.
Yet neither

of us speaks. Instead
we think of those
living there, others
who have died.
Your brother-in-law

has decided to emigrate:
the one sure escape.
As I draw up
at the lights, you droop
forward, hands on your lap.

4

The pubs are coming out.
In Dumbarton Rd
two drunks, having battered
each other senseless, sit
in their own vomit.

No-one interferes.
It is not easy
to accept there may
be a certain mercy
in living here.

The lights turn
to green. I imagine
you lying alone
in a white room, surrounded
by flimsy screens . . .

Stewart Conn, 1973   113

Political meeting, George Square, c.1929. Mitchell Library

Upper Clyde Shipbuilders work-in protest march, Glasgow Green, 1971. From left: Tony Benn (4), Willie Ross (5), Jimmy Reid (7). Oscar Marzaroli

ON JOHN MACLEAN

'I am not prepared to let Moscow dictate to Glasgow.'
Failures may be interesting, but it is the firmness
of what he wanted and did not want
that raises eyebrows: when does the quixotic
begin to gel, begin to impress, at what point
of naked surprise?
                                    'I for one will not follow
a policy dictated by Lenin until he knows
the situation more clearly.'
                                    Which Lenin hadn't time to,
and parties never did — the rock of nations
like the rock of ages, saw-toothed, half-submerged,
a cranky sputtering lighthouse somewhere, as often
out as lit, a wreck of ships all round,
there's the old barnacled 'Workingclass Solidarity',
and 'International Brotherhood' ripped open and awash,
while you can see the sleekit 'Great-Power Chauvinism'
steaming cannily past on the horizon
as if she had never heard of *cuius regio*.
Maclean wanted neither the maimed ships
nor the paradox of not wanting them
while he painfully trimmed the lighthouse lamp
to let them know that Scotland was not Britain
and writs of captains on the Thames
would never run in grey Clyde Waters.

Well, nothing's permanent. It's true he lost —
a voice silenced in November fog. Party
is where he failed, for he believed in people,
not in *partiinost'* that as everyone knows
delivers the goods. Does it? Of course.
And if they're damaged in transit you make do?
You do — and don't be so naive about this world!

Maclean was not naive, but
                                    'We are out
for life and all that life can give us'

was what he said, that's what he said.

Edwin Morgan, 1973

116   Unemployment protest march, Union Street, 1981. Glasgow Herald

BY THE PREACHING OF THE WORD

let gallows languish
let gas flurry
let glowworms fetch
let galluses flash
let geggies launch
let galoshes fish
let gasteropods munch
let gashes flinch
let glass vanish
let gases flush
let gaggles nourish
let goggles crunch
let Gagool fumble
let assegais frolic
let cargoes lurch
let Owlglass shuffle
let laughter urge
let lassies fudge
let lashes fash
let laggards finish
let Gardners furnish
let glasses varnish
let Gogol lunch
let grasses worry

let gags fashion
let sago munch
let gorgeous tundish
let garages burnish
let gorges brandish
let gargoyles forage
let gaffers ravage
let gavels hurry
let gravel crush
let gunwales crash
let grannies touch
let gurges famish
let gambols clinch
let gutters rush
let galaxies usher
let starfish grumble
let fungus gush
let gasmen gamble
let lurchers shamble
let gundogs fadge
let gasbags fuddle
let flunkeys gargle
let flags garnish
let Brasso furbish
LET GLASGOW FLOURISH

Edwin Morgan, 1974

Glasgow   coming home again

I found the garden had turned into a
naked yesterday soaked leafmould
yellow place
SUNFLOWERS WILTING

Took a train through the most industrial
part of my paradox; city under grey mist
Still, rust trees, rust heaps
of old cars dumped at the Kelvin estuary;
Brilliant fluorescent strip lights glowing
out from the Queen Mother hospital

Rain slow. Four o'clock on a Friday
is a special time for all these student
teachers waiting for the train home;
Tonight will be dancing and drinking

Saw a bus disguised as an Everton mint;
Could hardly believe my black and white striped vision
So stimulated by the city suddenly; then
I saw a man on a seat outside the library,
dead eyes staring at nothing

Betty lies on her back and rattles the hammer
The doctor said to humour her until
all the leaves had fallen off the trees!
So autumn seeps into us

Jean Milton, 1974

NEWS OF THE WORLD

As I came round by Templeton's
The sun was sliding low,
And every spire round Glasgow Green
Gave off its godly glow.

Deep in its rut the river shed
A skin of shit and scum,
And glinted through the fretted bridge,
Gold as Byzantium.

Then suddenly the sun was snuffed
Behind a sooty cloud,
And night let fall on Glasgow Green
Its sulphur-stinking shroud.

Black in its bed the river slinks
Down to the whining weir.
The yellow lamps along its banks
Come out — and with them, fear.
And fear floods out and fills the dark,
And the dark and the fear are one,
And standing on this bridge I know
The things that must be done.

For hardly fifty yards from here
Last night at half-past-ten
A Southside girl was gagged and shagged
By seven Brigton men.
And when the bully-boys were done,
They left her on the mud:
A crumpled stem and a crushed flower
And a dark splash of blood.

The slimy river secretly
Slid on, and far away
A furnace flared into the night
And the night was light as day.

A whistle shrilled. Across the Green
To London Road the men
Ran stumbling, and to hide their flight
The darkness dropped again.

But torchlight sliced the darkness where
She lay limp on the mud.
A crushed flower and a crumpled stem
And a dark splash of blood.
And torchlight fell on the twisted face
And it fell on the tangled hair.
On the clawed thighs, on the clenched fists
The torches threw their glare.
And then big Sean of Surrey Street
Came knifelike through the crowd,
And when he knew that it was true
He swore by holy blood
That he would hunt the bastards down
Had dibbled dirty seed,
And all their cheeks would grin like lips
And every throat would bleed.

Aye, well might the stinking river sink
As though in fear it fell.
And well might the rising sun burn red
As though it rose on hell.
For thirteen Southside men had sworn
To smear their blades with blood
For the crumpled stem and the crushed flower
And the red stain on the mud.

And now as I stand on the swaying bridge
Above the sluggish stream,
I know that a night of knives is down
And I know it is no dream.
My fingers clutch the greasy rail,
Frozen fast by fear.

A minute from the clanging street,
And yet I cannot stir.
And faint and far across the Green
To the grimy banks of Clyde
From the depths of the dark there twists a scream
Like a slow sword in the side.
Cry upon cry, and the crying rises,
Falls, and swells again,
And nearer, louder beat the drumming
Feet of running men,
Till close at hand the thud of feet
Is stilled. The shouting dies.
The furnace flares. The killing ground
Is framed beneath my eyes.

At the place on the path where it was done
Last night at half-past-ten,
Their blades ablaze like liquid light
Are seven Brigton men.

They stand like a glinting rock on the shore
As the tide creeps all around —
Thirteen crouching Southside men
Who move without a sound.

And they close on the men who stand on the spot
Where she lay sprawled on the mud.
A crumpled petal, a crushed stem,
And a dark splash of blood.

Is it only fear that holds me here
Where I stand on the bridge alone,
Though I know how a blade can slice as though
Through blubber to the bone?

A twisted face and tangled hair
And clawed thighs on the mud.
A crumpled stem and a crushed flower
And a dark splash of blood.

121

And a shaking scream from a broken boy
Is signal for the shock.
Cry upon cry. With a flashing surge
The sea is upon the rock.
A chalky face is crossed with red,
And again, again, again.
Behind the savage glitter of
A filed and flailing chain,
I see a boy go down on his back,
His muffler running red,
While the kid who killed him falls beside
Him, gashed across the head.

The furnace flames are curling low
And the dark returns at last,
And through the scream of fighting shrills
A piercing whistle blast.
And darkness drops on the Green again
And I move like a man in a dream —
A dream of hell — but knowing well
That things are what they seem.

Is there a man who never knew
A red mist mask his sight?
Is there a man who never knew
The joy I knew tonight?

As I came round by Templeton's
The sun was sliding low.
In a black night of black despair
From Glasgow Green I go.

Iain Hamilton, 1974

"TINY TUNES RULE ALL"

Wild rubbish, fine rubble and black broken windows —
six winters of hollow Glasgow and you're a wonder
of dereliction. You're sprayed and scribbled on the backs
of torn-off buildings. You're used confetti-coloured ˙
wallpaper peeling between hearth holes and old empty
door holes. You're a bored boy with a stack of
grudges. You're sharp noses, sharp eyes
steering the Lord's disapproval through uncountable curtains.
You're yesterday's plans not completed till tomorrow is
dying. You're the clash of class against class
so reverberant your nerves burst. You're a bottle of biddy.
You're a pint. You're a sack with a thirst.
You're a sick hack dropped from the mass.
You're put out to pasture in ash. And you're broken glass.

Anne Stevenson, 1974

SCHOOL FRIEND

A platform lad in a miracle world
  of gritty railway steam
    at Hyndland, Crow Road, Partick West,
he kept a penny Woolworth book
and captured all the engine names and numbers
    the beasts that panted every night
      within their glass and iron cages
        awaiting his command.

Saturday lunchtime "Any cigarette cards mister?"
to tram-borne clerks all homeward bound
for hot pies football cinemas
late night wireless by the fire
before the Sabbath sermon, the Botanic Garden stroll
cold ham and visitors to tea
when "Railway Engines of the World" was the series
at fifty cards the set.

Like a Daniel he had bathed
in furnace heat through the frosty air
footplate free in the city night
turntabled to death and glory
steel connecting rods his lances for the foe
and the great wheels four-four-o
his chariot against the weakness of the world.

Once in the dark of a dying suburb
he roamed the ruined Blackpool train
flat beer stale cake forgotten fags
and dodged the railway police who searched
like goblins in the foggy dark.

Once he sent the fussy nine-ten chattering
gallus locomotive of the gas-lamps
to some romantic rendezvous
of spies and sailors
in a far moon-haunted Clyde-coast town.

Then he was flicked from the sky
below a bombers' moon
and his time was stopped
above a foreign town
and the world quietly moved away
on its deterministic rails.

Fumbles now and then the dog-eared fading cards
    from the tin box by his bed
   as if they were a rosary;
    tells them over and over
  with the white tight gloves he wears
   to meet his love
   who never comes.

Bill McCorkindale, 1975

Bridges over the Clyde, c.1963. Oscar Marzaroli

125

A GUDE BUKE

Ah like a gude buke
a buke's aw ye need
jis settle doon
hiv a right gude read

Ay, a gude buke's rerr
it makes ye think
nuthin tae beat it
bar a gude drink

Ah like a gude buke
opens yir mine
a gude companion
tae pass the time

See me wi a buke, bit
in a bus ur a train
canny whack it
wee wurld i yir ain

Ay, ah like a gude buke
widny deny it
dje know thon wan
noo — whit dje cry it?

Awright, pal, skip it
awright, keep the heid
howm ah tae know
yir tryin tae read?

Stephen Mulrine, 1975

from ANGLES

3 Cathedral

One late summer day
Spent with you in
A touch too much of the sun.
Hot city and uncompromisingly
Glasgow. Warts and all.

Another grim cathedral.
Ghosts in a cold cold crypt.
Shadows where I left you cold
Cold insinuating to the bone.
Nothing was sacred really.

Outside the Necropolis
Clung crawling to the hill,
Urns and John Knox,
Thoughts of an ostentatious death.
I was terrified.

Oh I loved you in spite of
My tired feet in tight shoes.
Love made me numb. But
We were a poor match.
You found me ill fitting.

The Cathedral Church of St Mungo, 1969. George Oliver

The Necropolis, looking south, 1969. George Oliver

4 Hillhead

November: how it rained.
How it rained when
Fat and sad in black
I ran to your house,
Rang the bell and
Made a pretence of anger
Running up the stairs
To a room where
Your small hands shaped
Graceful words around you.

You had grown thin and brittle
Like a bird.
I could see your wings upon the wall.
My words flew out like feathers
To fleece them.
You meant to fly and
You were not afraid to fall.

Again outside
Against the soft hiss
Of rainy traffic,
Our quick breath smoked,
We passed by tattered leaves,
Dead rainbows in gutters,
We shared a last umbrella and
A cold cold kiss.

6 Now

Sometimes now
On my way to visit
Other friends
Who live in the same place,
I think that there
You live too.
And I cannot now
Even ring the bell
And climb the stair
To drink tea or pass
The time of day with you.

I wrecked our friendship
On love's precipitous reef.

Sometimes now
I lie awake and think
With a kind of shock
How I saw you
In Hillhead Station
And ran away
Up into the busy street.
Dear God. Even
The instinctive dogs stop
And sniff each other
When they meet.

Catherine Lucy Czerkawska, 1975

HEY YOO

It's love loosens yer tongue
even though ye really are
a narkie auld knocker.

Ye think it's hate, pal, but ye're wrang.

Ye care enough tae gie's yer patter.

Ah'm listenin:
any minute noo yoo an me's
goin tae get lyrical.

Nicol Cunningham, 1975

Meths drinkers near Paddy's Market, 1968. Oscar Marzaroli

DISCOVERY

"City! I am true son of thine;"
Alexander Smith

Tourists ken mair nor natives we are tellt
sae I hae returnt to Glasgow
on a day trip wi a wee guide book.

I stert wi the City Chambers; a masterpiece
of Victorian oppulence built at the height of the Imperial
period. It looks like the City Chambers
to me.

There's mair Victorian authenticity in St Vincent Street.
I peep into ane o the auld offices
I mind for smooth daurk mahogany desks
fittit wi ink wells and hie, wooden stools without backs
and daurk, important clerks bent owre huge, leather-bound books.
They've aa been modernised wi multi-colourt
girls.

The Cathedral I still find daurk and gloomy
— but shrunk.
Provand's Lordship, wi its museum, remains less to my taste
than The People's Palace on Glasgow Green
even if it's *still* Glasgow's auldest buildin.
The University has the same grand view out to the country
and again I dinna ken hou to get in.
Kelvingrove Art Gallery husnae lost
my favourite Degas and Rembrandt
nor Renfrew Street Charles Rennie Mackintosh's
Art School.

I'm no surprised to be tellt there's nae castle in
Castle Street or that "Greek" Thomson wisnae a Greek
— I gie his church a miss.

I ken about the Molendinar Burn up by the Cathedral
whaur, of course, St Mungo bathed and fished for salmon
— I thocht it had dried up
but we can aa learn something

— it's nou a "closed sewer"!

Duncan Glen, 1976

Glasgow Art Gallery and Museum from Kelvingrove Park, 1973. George Oliver

131

THE HERT O THE CITY

"In Glasgow, that damned sprawling evil town"
G.S. Fraser

I'm juist passin through
late at nicht. I risk a walk doun
through the gloomy tiled tunnel o Central Station
to Argyle Street and the Hielantman's Umbrella
for auld time's sake.

I see them at aince. Three girls and a wee fella
wi a bleedin heid. He's shakin wi laughter
and the bluid's splatterin on the shop windae.

I'm juist about awa back up the stairs when they're
aa round me. "On your ain?" "It's awfu cauld!"
"Ye shouldna be here by yersel!"

I canna help but notice the smell o drink and dirt.
His heid's a terrible sicht.

I look round but I *am* on my ain.
"Whaur are you from?" "Preston?" "You'll know Blackpool?"
Soon he'll hae my haill life story out o me.

"You maun be cauld" and
"Ye shouldna be here by yersel."

I offer them some money to get in out o the cauld
but they lauch at the idea. They're no hungry
and there's plenty wine left.

They'll get fixed up themorrow.
It's warm enough unner the brig.

They'd walk me back safe to my pletform
but the polis'll be in the station.

"Ye shouldna be here by yersel!"

132   **Duncan Glen,** 1976

SWEET CLYDE

"Wi mony a long and weary wimple,"
William Hamilton of Gilber*t*field

I was born here in Cam' slang
and nou I'm back
gey near a tourist.

I staun by the dirty, dirty banks o Clyde
doun river frae the "village"
near the warks
takin in the view.

There're mony wearie wimplin weys
o Clyde frae Leadhills to Cam'slang
but here it beats aa for bends in the river.

You'd near think it would turn back on itsel
haein had a taste o what's to come.

Duncan Glen, 1976

BRINDISI (Catullus 27)

Gies another blast a that
dubble strength
an full the mug
Toass the watter doon the sink
throw away the watter jug
Keep Postumia's party gaun
gie Postumia wan is well

somedy help ur up, she's fell

David Neilson, 1976

THE BUTCHERS OF GLASGOW

The butchers of Glasgow have all got their pride
But they'll tell you that Willie's the prince
For Willie the butcher he slaughtered his wife
And he sold her for mutton and mince

It's a terrible story to have to be telt
And a terrible thing to be done
For what kind of man is it slaughters his wife
And sells her a shilling a pun

For lifting his knife and ending her life
And hanging her high like a sheep
You widnae object but you widnae expect
He wid sell the poor woman so cheap

But the Gallowgate folk were delighted
It didnae cause them any tears
They swore that Willie's wife Mary
Was the best meat he'd sold them for years

Matt McGinn, 1976

THIS UNRUNG BELL

This is the tree that never grew
This is the bird that never flew
This is the fish that never swam
This is the bell that never rang

What bloodless abortion silenced this unrung bell
split and cracked its gold;
and who can break the spell?

What unholy love or violence breaks pell-mell
to crumbling ash untouched and cold;
what bloodless abortion silenced this unrung bell?

The mythical bird that never flew or fell
perched dumb and yet had wings to fold;
and who can break her spell?

Dumb upon a rootless tree compelled
into what rich or barren idol;
what bloodless abortion silenced this unrung bell?

By what unperfected potent heaven or hell
are those iced and burning fins controlled;
and what rituals can break his spell?

What thick or buried obsessions creep, dispel
the ruin of love or death leaves all untold;
what bloodless abortion silenced this unrung bell?
And who can break the spell?

Neil McLellan, 1977

IN MEMORIAM — ANDERSTON

The music itself is better on the hi-fi.
You can isolate it with no disturbance
From the squalor of Anderston.
Here the sign should be neon lit "BINGO"
Not dull painted plywood "CONCERT HALL".

Inside the eye is pulled away by copper tympani,
Functional sweeps of shining horns,
Dappled fiddles, cellos and fat basses,
Elegant sophisticated woodwinds,
Monkey suits, beards and black gowns
All under the sharp clean lights.   135

'Hey mate! Look at the big blond bit
In the second row of the violins.
How about the wee dolly with the oboe?'

Now some music. Mozart — or was it Mahler?
Then the interval, outside, next door
Beside the ring road chaos.
"Two large Bells Jimmy and two Exports"
In the corner desperate with some misery
A head in hands and vomit on the boards.

Inside again on upright hard backed seats
Watching and listening
As Menuhin builds surely through the Beethoven cadenza,
And in a quiet stretch
A jet boosts over up from Abbotsinch.

The music itself is better on the hi-fi at home.
You have an easy chair and no distractions.

Tom Berry, 1977

GORBALS

Spence and Matthew manufactured
Concrete cliffs shape the new Gorbals.
But the old culture survives on odd brick fragments
Liberated into sight by the aerosol.
CUMBIES, TONGS and TOIS
Record their war cries
In strangely elegant graffiti
With the spiderspun delicacy
Of a Steinberg drawing.

A fine tall looping 'C'
A fat short 'U' and the other letters
Mark that the CUMBIES passed this way.

Other factions intertwine and overcross
In a lacework of white on rusty brick
Against the grey of the carefully calculated new tenements.

But this is all accident,
Part of this accidental city.

Tom Berry, 1977

THE BARGAIN

The river in January is fast and high.
You and I
are off to the Barrows.
Gathering police-horses twitch and fret
at the Tron end of London Road and Gallowgate.
The early kick-off we forgot
has us three-thirty rubbing the wrong way
against all the ugly losers
getting ready to let fly
where the two rivers meet.

January
and we're looking back   looking forward
don't know which way.

But the boy with the three
beautiful bakelite
Bush radios for sale in Meadow's minimarket is
buttonpopping stationhopping he
doesn't miss a beat   sings along   it's easy
to every changing tune.

Yes today we're in love aren't we?
with the whole splintering city
its big quick river   wintry bridges
its brazen black Victorian heart.

137

So what if every other tenement
wears its hearth on its gable end
all I want
is my glad eye to catch
a glint in your flinty Northern face again
just once.   Oh I know it's cold
and coming down
and no we never lingered long among the Shipbank traders.
Paddy's Market   underneath the arches
stank too much today —
the usual wetdog reek
rising from piles of old damp clothes.
Somebody absolutely steamboats he says on sweet warm wine
swigged plaincover from a paperbag
squats in a puddle with nothing to sell
but three bent forks   a torn
calendar (last year's)
and a single broken plastic sandal.
So we hadn't the stomach for it today.
Oh you could say
we don't deserve a bargain then.
No connoisseur can afford to be too scrupulous
about keeping his hands clean.
There was no doubt   the rare   the beautiful
and the bugle-beaded   the real antique   dirt cheap
among the rags and drunks
you could easily take to the cleaners.

At the Barrows though everything has its price
no haggling   believe me
this boy knows his radios.
Pure Utility
and what that's worth these days.
Suddenly the Fifties are fashionable
and anything within a decade of art deco
a rarity you'll pay through the nose for.
The man with the patter and all these curtain lengths

Paddy's Market, 1969. Oscar Marzaroli

The 'Barras', 1968. Oscar Marzaroli

139

in fibreglass is flabbergasted at the bargain
and says so in so many words.
Jesus every other
arcade around here's
a Fire Surround Boutique. —

We watch one struggling family
father carrying hearth home
mother wound up with kids.
All the couples we know
fall apart or have kids.
Oh we've never shouldered much
we'll stick to small ikons
(as long as they're portable) for our home —
a dartboard   a peacock feather
a stucco photoframe.

We queue in the blue
blue haze of hot fat
for Danny's Do-nuts that grit
our teeth with granulated sugar.
I lose you and find you
lose you again.
Now two stalls away you thumb
through a complete set of manuals for primary teachers from
the nineteen-thirties.
I rub my sleeve
on a dusty Chinese saucer
till the gilt shows through.
Oh come on   we promised
we'd not let our affection for the slightly cracked
trap us into such expenditure again.
Oh even if it is a bargain
we won't buy.
The stallholder says we'll be the death of her.
She says   see January
it's been the doldrums the day.

And it's packing up time
with the dark coming early
and as cold as the river.
At the bus-stop I show you
the beady bag and the maybe rosewood box
with the inlaid butterfly and the broken catch.
You've bought
a record by the Shangri-Las
a pinstripe waistcoat that needs a stitch
it just won't get   and a book called "Enquire
Within — Upon Everything".
The raw cold gets colder.
There doesn't seem to be a lot to say.
I wish we could either mend things
or learn to throw them away.

Liz Lochhead, 1977

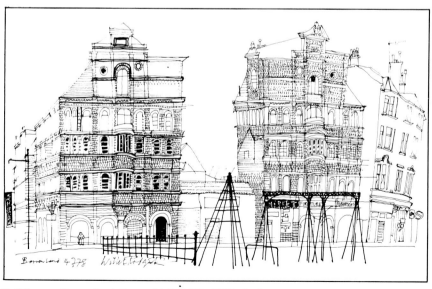

Buildings at Barrowland. Pen and ink, 1978. Willie Rodger

GLASCHU

AHOY! Glasgow seen from sea or air
a gutted city inhabited by gnomes
houses lined up along its quays
night-watchmen's fires and vegetable ships.

AHOY! Agog I first saw light behind
blinds in a hulk of staggering battered streets,
a record of buying and selling wreckage
that smelt of psychiatric alcohol.

Hearing a dog bark up a cobbled lane
as back-courts played their drollery of blows
the child I was climbed spikes to nowhere;
my circus pummelled Punch-and-Judy shows.

Skeletal bridges gallop over roads
jet-set with oilskins, coal and umbrellas
that eddy backward here and there in time
bubbles and mushrooms blackening on streams.

Under ears of wheat glistering on water
and sunlight cutting into orange peel
my Clyde proves to be swirling backward too
now mist brings dissolution to its ships.

J.F. Hendry, 1978

142   Hydepark Street, Anderston, 1962. Oscar Marzaroli

THE BROOMIELAW

Time, time, what was time?
The empty stare of a wide wide square
in a sprawling rudimentary city;
deserted streets of poverty and pride
full of criminal sincerity:
docks and barriers; a throng
pursuing us in the shape of birds
like hovering unemployment,
the public burden for which is no atonement;
the circulation of money, like a sin.

Time, time, what was time?
A great Trade Fair. A holiday air
on the lower reaches of the Clyde:
a floral bandstand in the rain:
the interval between each act,
sudden blindness in the stalls,
never the dancer with the loving eyes
in a world of analysis
but isolation and recall to all we lacked:
the pipe, the drum, the inward rage.

Time, time, what was time?
A dosshouse, where a ruined millionaire
gambled away humanity:
a neighbourhood of trundled misery,
no one staying long enough to see
the outrage and the agony:
good-bye to love, the one romantic gesture
none could hold for long;
Bedlam, where love broke her heart and died,
but no one said a word because of pride.

J.F. Hendry, 1978

AT CENTRAL STATION

At Central Station, in the middle of the day,
a woman is pissing on the pavement.
With her back to the wall and her legs spread
she bends forward, her hair over her face,
the drab skirt and coat not even hitched up.
Her water hits the stone with force
and streams across into the gutter.
She is not old, not young either,
not dirty, yet hardly clean,
not in rags, but going that way.
She stands at the city centre, skeleton at the feast.
Executives off the London train
start incredulously but jump the river
and meekly join their taxi queue.
The Glasgow crowd hurries past,
hardly looks, or hardly dares to look,
or looks hard, bold as brass, as
the poet looks, not bold as brass
but hard, swift, slowing his walk
a little, accursed recorder, his feelings
as confused as the November leaves.
She is a statue in a whirlpool,
beaten about by nothing he can give words to,
bleeding into the waves of talk
and traffic awful ichors of need.
Only two men frankly stop,
grin broadly, throw a gibe at her
as they cross the street to the betting-shop.
Without them the indignity,
the dignity, would be incomplete.

Edwin Morgan, 1978

Maryhill. Aquatint, c.1961. Thomas Walsh

MARYHILL

1

There's a space where that building was.
What was there before? A big black tenement?
I can't remember. It's just that
suddenly I notice it isn't there.
I'm sure it was there yesterday.
You can see right across to Summerston now.
And further beyond to the Campsies.

The mothers in a gaggle outside the school gate.
A queue against the railings for the 60 bus.
Leather jacket. Jeans.
High heels. Mascara.
Mammy with wean. Mr with newspaper.
Cigarette. Cigarette. A pipe. A poet.
The inspector crosses the road from the garage,
notepad and pencil and checking his watch.
Everyone looks up the road.

The strike is over.
Inside the low-roofed utility building,

Maryhill. Aquatint, 1940s. Charles Murray

146   Maryhill, 1980. Ken MacGregor

the children fold, unfold their arms.
Brother Jerome commences the lessons
for yet another day.

> But there's a space where that building was.

2

    Out of the dark close she comes
onto the street, her bright blue suit and hat
striking sharply on the atmosphere, a vibrant signal
on a cold clear afternoon. Against her shoulder and her breast
the white shape of the shawl, the baby's head, its back supported
through layers by a firm blue glove. She has that bustling,
wrapped round, straight from hospital look, the hat and suit
have been waiting for this day. Blue. She took a chance on it.

Her taxi waits. She enters with a gracious smile
that shows she knows she's VIP
and gives an elegant regal wave
to her old pair of fans at the upstairs window.
The taximan drives off like the proudest of chauffeurs.
Something tells me it's a boy. Her first.

3

Soft brown hat, dark blue jacket, double-breasted,
a neat white triangle in his top pocket,
he has to hold on to the railing
moves very slowly
as he comes down the steps
through the gate and out on to the street
where he stands, considering, a letter in his hand,
then turns himself, so definite each movement,
around, to face
the pillar box —

just fifty yards or so
further up the street
but for him
a major excursion.

He walks on to the road
peering from left to right
through wispy spectacles.
But now he walks more easily.
The problem with the legs
is only when walking
downstairs.

4

Yowling down the hill
hand to his forehead
then to his arm
as if to test
if it is broken,
then back to his forehead
where the pain is most intense,
the brain.

"Threw me o'er that wa' . . .
It's near eight feet.
Ah hit ma heid oan concrete.
Aw naw! Ma watch!
Lookit ma new watch!
It's broken!"

Having to go home at night
and explain.

5

Spiderwebs of snow. Branches low.
Boots crunch deep. Cold powder. Damp ankles.

Heavy black marks — tracks of a man
along the riverbank where no trout lie
no salmon leap up from the sea.

Twigs crack. Prints of paws and claws.
Ice splinters. A coffin of snow
askew on a bench.

Wood. Brick. Weeds in shattered windows.
Old torn face patched and streaked with snow
hangs down dark and tattered
towards the water. His ghosts gone now.
They left no clues.

High arches. Redundant railway bridge.
Deserted signal box. Disused canal.
Suddenly, the highrise flats.
Bustle of traffic.
Up on the road, the snow has turned to slush,
things have gone slippery underfoot,
the early dark seeps in.
The windows of the pubs light up
prepared for opening time.

This time. This place. These people.
This specific set against the snow
is not exactly paradise.

6

Last year white trousers
both sexes, then the shorn and spiky look of punk,
shivering through the streets in paper shirts,
trying to look vicious but raising smiles;
this year the girls in long floral dresses,
laced at the hem, unfeminist,
the boys, sons of Travolta-hype,
greasing their hair like pale-ghost Teds.

Teenagers gather round the entrances and empty streets
of housing estates at night
as if waiting for something invisible to happen,
Captain Impossible to descend from the sky,
their youth to be fulfilled.

But nothing happens.
For them there is no past.
The highrise towers light up the skyline.
Radio Clyde 261.

7

Cigarette between lips,
eyes squinting through years of smoke,
white stubble like a hedgehog,
Tony hasn't shaved today or yesterday.
Knocks down the Corn Flakes from the top shelf,
plonks a pound of butter on the counter,
cuts some cheese, bends forward to hear small voices,
collects pennies, hands out sweets,
stands at the till to count it up,
looking down the line as he hands out change
— "Gies a boatle o ginger, Tony" —
Starts again.

8

Yellow light splashes out from the chippie
like sawdust on the pavement.

Black and white checked hatbands,
long dark coats, caps pulled down to nose
to hide the eyes, four policemen
shove a man against the window.
A cat looks out.
Gloved hands pushing
ask gruff questions.

His friend is lifted
at the bus stop
carrying a bulky parcel
that stinks of vinegar.

Glint of handcuffs, wrist to wrist,
hauled down into the kerbside Panda

— "Ah've goat tae get hame.
    Ah've left four weans.
    Their mother's oan the nightshift."

— "Aye? Well we'll dae yae fur that yin tae."

Free hand loses grip
as the car door closes
and the parcel spills out
leaving a trail of fish and chips
in the gutter as they go.

9

Shops closed down
their windows boarded
to make way for the motorway
that never happened.
A tree grows out a chimney.
Streets crisscross, divert, make bends
round the spaces where the buildings were.
Now that they've gone, we want them back,
but it wasn't exactly paradise, if you remember.
The past is always picturesque. The great dark fractured
glass-eyed ruins of rats and winos
give Gothic thrills viewed through car windows,
or caught, glowering on their muddy banks,
cracked patterns and puddles, spilled trashcans and all,
glimmering in the subtle halflight of a Joan Eardley canvas;
but the present needs more substance.

Tom McGrath, 1979   151

GASOMETER FOLLIES
(for Edwin Morgan)

Demolishers always leave some bits
behind (adding, like sculptors, by subtraction) —
an arch, a ragged tenement-end, a stac
of rubble in a field of blaes —
either out of a kind of urban politeness
or as advertisement or memento,
a remembrance of things that were
or to be, like uneaten food on a Roman table.

Will future cities build such crazy graces
into their windscaled landscapes:
rusty constructions, uncrumbled concrete ruins,
focal points of twisted girders, steel drum
copses, the odd Finnieston Crane —
morsels for the excavators
of a new age?

Hamish Whyte, 1981

152   Finnieston Crane, 1975. Ken MacGregor

THE MITCHELL LIBRARY

1

I dreamed last night I saw Atlantis drown
without effort (there were no straining people who wanted
to breathe their proper element),
it was as casual as falling asleep.
Now, in this great brain (its thoughts are paper,
its cells are high rooms with difficult ceilings)
I am inclined over a desk by a window.
Everything imagined is catalogued —
A ... At ... Atlantis ... *New Atlantis* by
Francis Bacon, London, 1626.
Kings make their linear way to defeat.
The nitrogen cycle turns and involves,
even, the bodies of Kings.
All this, the mumbling, diligent library notes.
Sand is anatomised, grass is remembered.
Let us say,
'This is chaos and here is its index.'

2

In a rich man's life the purlieus
and lineaments of his behaviour
follow only his own plan.
Nor can a great library err.
At the front, this one surmounts
its dark and earnest stone
with a green dome like a bright idea.
At the back, a cack-handed
run of inscriptions (RAPHAEL   WATT   M. ANGELO
NEWTON   FLAXMAN) suggests an order
I can relish failing to grasp.

Kevin McCarra, 1982   153

JINGLE

This is the bell that never rang

This
RANG
This is
RANG RANG
This is the bell
RANG
This is the bell that
RANG
This is never
RANG
This is never the bell that
RANG
This is the rang bell
RANG RANG RANG
This is the bell that
RANG RANG RANG RANG
                never

This is the tree that never grew

This tree never grew green
This green tree never grew
Neverever green grew this tree
This tree grew never evergreen

This is the bird that never flew

this is the
        bird
this is the
        bird
this wee
        bird
teenie
        bird
totie
        bird
chookie
        bird
this is the
        bird
it never
        flew
  never
        flew
  never
        flew
  never
        flew
  aw!

This is the fish that never swam

this is the fish
tell me who I am
fish out of water
never ever swam

Alan Spence, 1982

G.M. HOPKINS IN GLASGOW

(For J.A.M.R.)

Earnestly nervous yet forthright, melted
by bulk and warmth and unimposed rough grace,
he lit a ready fuse from face to face
of Irish Glasgow. Dark tough tight-belted
drunken Fenian poor ex-Ulstermen
crouched round a brazier like a burning bush
and lurched into his soul with such a push
that British angels blanched in mid-amen
to see their soldier stumble like a Red.
Industry's pauperism singed his creed.
He blessed them, frowned, beat on his hands. The load
of coal-black darkness clattering on his head
half-crushed, half-fed the bluely burning need
that trudged him back along North Woodside Road.

Edwin Morgan, 1983

FETCH ON THE FIRST OF JANUARY

Nae time eftir the Bells, and the
New Year new in wi' the
usual crowd, wi' whisky, cheers and kisses —
Ah'd aboot managed the windaes shut
some clown had thrown wide
hopin' tae hear the hooters on the Clyde
when the door went.
           Well, well,
who'd've thought Ah'd be staunin' there
tae first foot masel'?

This some kinuffa Huntigowk for Hogmanay?
Hell-mend-ye, ye're
a bad penny, Jimmy —
Mister Ne'erdy Ne'er-do-weel
sae chitterin' ill-clad for the caul'
sae drawn an' pale,
oh, wi' the black bun burnin' a hole
in yir poackit an' the coal
a Live Coal.

'Gawn, get' — Ah should shout it,
should shake a stick or ma fist,
Oh but Ah should hunt ye, by Christ,
the wey you chased that big black tyke
that dogged ye wance, mind? —
A' the wey fae Hope Street hame.

Ah'll no let ye near me,
don't make me laugh,
got a much better
Better Half.
Och, aye tae glower at each other
was tae keek in a gey distortin' mirror,
yet ye've the neck tae come back again
wi yir bare face, Jake Fetch,
the image o' my ain?
Ice roon yir mooth when ye kiss me,
the cauld plumes o' yer breath —
Ah'm lukkin' daggers
you're lukkin' like Death.
Ah'm damned if ye'll get past ma door,
nae fear!

Come away in, stranger, Happy New Year.

Liz Lochhead, 1983

SONG FOR GLASGOW
(to the tune of Jamie Raeburn's Farewell)

Night-lights on the river
partners in the dance
we're settled here together
in the seed-bed of romance
you've sometimes been a saviour
rarely been my curse
but we can shape the future now
for better or for worse

While others flaunt their splendour
in the rivalries of trade
they've no resource of humour
just some finery displayed
their glory's all in fashion
attractive to the eye
but your heart beats with passion
that spills into my life

We've known fears and deprivation
in the waste-lands of our dreams
we've been forged by politicians
their dealings and their schemes
but love's domain is beauty
and lovers raise a home
so I'll celebrate my city
in the days that are to come

Alasdair Robertson, 1983

Glasgow and the Clyde; looking over Queen's Dock. Mitchell Library

NOTES

Sources for the poems, biographical and bibliographical notes, etc.

Page 7

"Glasgow". From *City Poems*, 1857. A romantic poem about Glasgow, but one which admits the intrusion of "Black Labour" and trains that plunge and shriek: this is a city where the sunset vies with the furnace, a place of "haunting joy or anguish". The poem is full of Grimshaw-like scenes and gemmy phrases ("Smoulder in smoky sunsets, flare/ on rainy nights") which evoke mid-nineteenth century Glasgow in its industrial glory and squalor — a city of contrasts, as indeed it still is — in Edwin Morgan's words, "the weird, fibrous chiaroscuro of Glasgow".

A suitable poem to introduce a collection of modern Glasgow poems, it takes the city seriously as a poetic subject, in form, content and language — as it was not to be for three quarters of a century, being instead overgrown by kailyard and mocked by music hall — a legacy regrettably still with us. However, Smith's poem has echoes yet, a hundred years later, in such poems as "Northern Nocturnal" (*New Poems* 1955) and "Night Pillion" by Edwin Morgan.

19

"Exhibition Ode, No. III". From *Glasgow Exhibition Odes and Lyrics*, 1901. A McGonagallish effusion on the Glasgow International Exhibition of 1901, held in Kelvingrove Park: inaugurating a glorious new century of Glaswegian Industry and Commerce. Also in this volume is a poem on that peculiar idiom, "Kelvinside English".

19, 21

Charles Joseph Kirk's "Ode to the Clyde" and "Glasgow Types" were first printed in *Glasgow University Magazine* (GUM) and reprinted in *Glasgow University Verses 1903-1910* and in his *Clyde Ballads*, 1911. The illustrations by OH! are the work of his friend James Bridie (O.H. Mavor). "Ode to the Clyde" was written in the cage of a buoy moored in the Clyde off Cardross.

26

The idea for "I Belong to Glasgow" is supposed to have come to Will Fyffe from seeing a drunk man in Central Station fumbling for his train ticket and crying, "I belong to Glasgow — and Glasgow belongs to me!"

27

"Nuns in Gordon Street". From *The Wise Men Come to Town* (Gowans & Gray, 1923). One of the few serious Glasgow poems of the first quarter of the century; it could be compared with Tom Leonard's "A Priest came on at Merkland Street" of nearly 50 years later (in his *Poems*, 1973). Jeffrey, who worked on the staff of the *Evening Times* and *Glasgow Herald*, also wrote *Fantasia Written in an Industrial Town* (1933) — not Glasgow as such but an amalgam of towns of the industrial belt.

30

John F. Fergus was a much-respected medical man in Glasgow, friend of Lister. "The Yairds" is from the Glasgow Ballad Club fourth collection of members' work, *Ballads and Poems*, 1924.

31
"Glesca'". From *Dandie and Other Poems* (Gowans & Gray, 1925). Glasgow through the eyes of a country visitor.

33
"In Glasgow" is from MacDiarmid's epoch-making first collection of poems, *Sangschaw* (Blackwood, 1925). F.G. Scott is the composer Francis George Scott.

34
"Glasgow Street" originally appeared in *Via* (Boriswood, 1933). The arrangement of the lines has been recently altered by the author.

34
"The women talk . . ." has never been included in any collection of Muir's poems. It is taken from the Glasgow section of *Scottish Journey* (Heinemann/Gollancz, 1935; reissued by Mainstream, 1979) — his "graphic report on the present and his bold plans for Scotland's future." (blurb) He wrote: "as I can speak with no exact knowledge of the rich of Glasgow, I shall give instead a short poem which took shape during my journey through the industrial regions, and arose from a sense of the violent contrasts that I saw on every side." (p. 152) Readers of Muir's *Autobiography* will know the terrible part played by Glasgow in his personal mythology.

35
An answer to "Glasgow, 1960" is given by Edwin Morgan in his Glasgow Sonnet iv (1972).

36
Luis Cernuda was appointed lecturer in Spanish at Glasgow University in January 1939 and remained in Glasgow until 1943. "Cementerio de la Ciudad" was first published in *Las nubes* (Buenos Aires, 1943). Edwin Morgan has also translated this poem (in 1956) — see his *Rites of Passage,* 1976. This version is from Ronald Butlin's *Creatures Tamed by Cruelty* (EUSPB, 1979).

37
from "Glasgow": for the various chunks of diatribe on Glasgow refer to the *Complete Poems 1920-1976.* The sorting out of MacDiarmid's writing on Glasgow is complicated by his habit of inserting sections of one poem in another — like making up jig-saws — MacDiarmid was no respecter of his text. Even this version of "Glasgow" (from *Voice of Scotland* June 1947) has been edited from a much longer piece — and the surgery approved by MacDiarmid.

41
"Night Pillion". From *Saltire Review* Autumn 1957. Foreshadowing of his future Glasgow poems. Hitherto uncollected.

42
"Rain in Sauchiehall Street." From *Honour'd Shade,* an anthology celebrating the bicentenary of Burns's birth, 1959.

44
"Glasgow Beasts". One of the most famous and funniest pieces of modern Glasgow poetry — and influential in its use of Glasgow speech — on Tom

Leonard in particular. First published in 1961 by the Wild Hawthorn Press, it ran to at least five editions. It is reprinted in the schools anthology *Ring of Words* (1970) but without the illustrations — papercuts by John Picking and Pete McGinn, which are reproduced here, reduced in scale and in different positions.

Incidentally, Garscadden Road is not "oot Polmadie" — presumably the names were chosen for their sound etc and not their geographical contiguity.

49
"Cod Liver Oil and Orange Juice". Also known as "Hairy Mary" or "Hairy Mary and the Hard Man". Despite other claims, this is the definitive version, now a classic in Scottish folk-song repertoire.

50–58
"To Joan Eardley". Although an incomer, as an artist Eardley certainly caught something of tenement life, especially in her paintings of children. This was the first of the famous group of Edwin Morgan's Glasgow poems (by which he is still unfortunately best known — at least in schools) written between April 1962 and September 1964. Five are printed here. Others include "Linoleum Chocolate", "Good Friday" and the over-anthologised "In the Snack-Bar". These are the poems, described by Morgan in an interview, "about simple things happening in Glasgow to me or other people or about things I read about in the paper." This "direct, realistic poetry" marked a change in his poetic direction and in that of a younger generation of writers. For his whole range see *Poems of Thirty Years* (Carcanet, 1982).

59
"The Glasgow Underground" was written for *Dick MacWhittie*, the Citizens' Theatre Christmas show, 1963, with music by Ian Gourlay. Since the modernisation of the Underground in the late 1970s some of the station names have been changed: Partick Cross is now Kelvin Hall and Copeland Rd. is Ibrox.

60
"glasgow's full of artists". Typical edinburgh remark. From *All Fall Down* (Kevin Press, 1965).

60
Other Glasgow poems by Kenneth White include "Song of the Coffin Close", "Zone" and "Ballad of the C. & W." (in *The Cold Wind of Dawn*, 1966, as is "Glasgow Night") and "Glasgow" (in *The Most Difficult Area*, 1968).

61
This is the first publication of "This is my Story". From the second series of "Television Poems" produced by Finlay J. Macdonald for BBC Scotland in 1967. See article by Macdonald, "Poets' Places", *Akros* 8, August 1968.

69
"Six Glasgow Poems". Tom Leonard's best known work. By the time "The Good Thief" appeared in *Scottish International* 1, January 1968, the sequence had been completed. Tom Leonard tried to publish them in *GUM*, which he then edited, but the printer refused to print them. "I then typed them up on a foolscap sheet and had this reproduced on a banda machine in the Student Representative Council offices. Then I put it as an insert into the issue of the

magazine when it appeared . . . The carry-on with the printers then reminds me that later for other Glasgow dialect poems a printer wanted 'foreign language rates'." (Tom Leonard in letter to editor) The poems are reprinted in Tom Leonard's *Poems* (1973) along with literal English translations.

71
"Glasgow Sabbath". In *Poems 1969 – 1972* (Poni Press) but written in 1967.

72
"The Coming of the Wee Malkies" is one of the most talked-about poems in Glasgow ever since it won 4th place in the BBC Scottish Home Service University Notebook Poetry Competition and was printed in *GUM*, Whitsun 1967. Controversy still rages as to who or what the Malkies are.

75
"The Jeely Piece Song". Another piece of modern Glasgow folklore, by singer and expert on children's songs and street ballads, Adam McNaughtan. Originally called "The Height Starvation Song". See also his poem "Are These Things Still Here?" *(Glasgow Herald* 24 April 1975) and his article on children's street songs, "Too old at eleven" *Chapbook* 4:1, 1968.

76
"Glasgow Nocturne". From *Lines Review* 26, Summer 1968.

77
"the docks on Sunday". From *GUM* 80:3, 1969 (with 13 other poems). For only five years, before she moved to Cornwall in 1974, Jean Milton's short "open verse" poems of life in (mainly) Glasgow appeared sporadically in the Scot. Lit. magazines. To read them is like reading a journal, but without any feelings of intrusion — the experience is shared.

79
"Rider". In *Scottish International* 8, November 1969. Appropriately, this deals with Glasgow poets and the difficulties of their emergence.

83
"Glasgow". From *Lines Review* 29, June 1969.

84
"In Glasgow". From *Twelve Songs* (Castlelaw Press, 1970).

86
"Nostalgie". Published in *Poems*, No. 10 in Duncan Glen's Parklands Poets series.

88
"Obituary". First appeared in the Glasgow University Extra Mural magazine, *EMU*, No.1, 1971 and was included, as was "Something I'm Not", in Liz Lochhead's best-selling collection, *Memo for Spring* (Reprographia, 1972).

90
"Charing Cross". In *New Edinburgh Review* 12, May 1971.

91
"Glasgow Sonnets". These were written 2-10 January 1972 and issued as a pamphlet by the Castlelaw Press in May of that year.

96
"By Kelvin Water". In *Lines Review* 42 & 43, September 1972 — February
1973.

129
"Hey Yoo". *Akros* 29, December 1975.

130, 132, 133
The three Duncan Glen poems were written in April 1976 and included in *Traivellin Man: a sequence o poems* (Akros, 1977).

133
"Brindisi". *Akros* 37, April 1978. A collection of these translations, *XII from Catullus,* was published by the Mariscat Press in 1982.

134
"The Butchers of Glasgow". One of McGinn's urban folk-songs. Many others, such as "The Ballad of John Maclean" and "The Red Yo Yo" are now part of the repertoire.

134
"This Unrung Bell." *Akros* 37, April 1977.

135
"In Memoriam — Anderston" and "Gorbals". Both from *Akros* 37, April 1977.

137
"The Bargain". "I think of it as a rewrite of *Obituary* ten years on in a way" (Liz Lochhead). From *Asphalt Garden* 4, 1977.

142, 143
"Glaschu" and "The Broomielaw". Included in *A World Alien* (Borderline, 1980).

144
"At Central Station". *Akros* 38, August 1978.

145
"Maryhill". *Words* 8, 1979.

152
"Gasometer Follies". Suggested by a conversation with Edwin Morgan about the Anniesland Gasometer. From *Cencrastus* 8, Spring 1982.

153
"The Mitchell Library". Published here for the first time.

154
"Jingle". From *Glasgow Zen* (Glasgow Print Studio, 1982).

155
"G.M. Hopkins in Glasgow". Gerard Manley Hopkins was in Glasgow August — October 1881. Two months later he wrote: "My Liverpool and Glasgow experience laid upon my mind a conviction, a truly crushing conviction, of the misery of town life to the poor and more than to the poor . . . of the degradation even of our race, of the hollowness of this century's civilisation: it made even life a burden to me to have daily thrust upon me the things I saw". From Edwin Morgan's "Sonnets from Scotland" (a work in progress). Published here for the first time.

155
"Fetch on the First of January". Published here for the first time.

157
"Song for Glasgow". Hitherto unpublished. Alasdair Robertson: musician; writer of lyrics for the umquhile Glasgow band, Cado Belle; now co-runs shop
164 in Glasgow specialising in folk records.

Gardner Street, Partick; Glasgow tenement restoration, 1983. George Oliver

Gorbals kids climbing in back court, 1963. Oscar Marzaroli

165

GLOSSARY of names and words as used in the text

barkit	besmeared
baudrons	cat
bevvying	drinking
biddy	cheap potent wine
bien	thriving, comfortable
biggin	house
birl't	revolved
bloo'er (blooter)	smash
bogey, the gemme's a	stalemate
broo	social security office (bureau)
burnty	burned-out house
causey	street (causeway)
caw	pull, knock over
chap	knock
chitterin'	shivering
chuckies	small stones, pebbles
cleg	horsefly
Clenny	Cleansing Department
cogs	wooden bowls
cowped	upended into (coup — a place for emptying loads of earth, ashes, rubbish, etc.)
crack	chat, gossip
curdy	farthing
daunerin'	strolling
dayligaun	twilight
didgy	dustbin
dod	lump, piece
douce	modest, gentle
dowie	mournful
dreep	let one's self down (a wall, for example) perpendicularly
drouthy	thirsty
dunner't	dead-beat
dunny	lower back passage (of close)
duntin'	banging
ettled	intended
fairfochen	exhausted
fankled	tangled
fash	worry, vex
fornent	against
free-the-bed	children's game (see *Scottish National Dictionary* under 'free-the-den')
166 *fyled*	defiled

galloglasses	warriors
gallus	devil-may-care
geggies	wooden street theatre booths
gemme's a bogey, the	stalemate
gey	very, "pretty"
girds	hoops
Glasgow magistrates	plump red herrings
glaur	muck, dirt
gully	"probably as in knife, 'half-shut', folding like a three foot rule" (Tom Wright)
hauf-bilet	half-boiled
hems, pit the, oan	put out of action, contain
hen	term of endearment (female)
hunch-cuddy(-hunch)	children's game (see *Scottish National Dictionary*)
hunkered	squatting on the haunches
huntygowk	April fool
jaloose	guess
jaw	abusive or insolent talk
jeely piece	jam sandwich
joukit	dodged
keelies	corner boys
Lennox	Bobby Lennox, Celtic footballer
lift	sky
lippen	trust, depend on
lumber	a girl to take home from the dancing (also verb)
maiks	halfpennies
midgie	small mosquito
minnie	minnow
nyafs	smart-alecks, wee nuisances (knaves)
oxter	armpit
Paradise	nickname for Celtic F.C.'s ground
pechin'	panting
peever	hopscotch
piece	sandwich
pit the hems oan	put out of action, contain
plankt	hidden
poky hats	ice-cream cones
Quinn, Jimmy	famous Celtic footballer
Reid	Jimmy Reid, Upper Clyde Shipbuilders trade union leader
rid	red
rone pipe	pipe for carrying off rain water
sannies	sandshoes
sapsy	sonsy
scaurs	cliffs

screwtaps	beer bottles with screw tops
scunners	objects of loathing
shauchlin	shuffling
shilpit	thin, starved-looking
shootin the craw	making an escape
siver	gutter
skitin'	flying off at speed in a slanting direction
slevvery	wet, damp
smore	choke
stank	drain
sneckit	caught
soor-dook	buttermilk
soss	mess
speir'd	asked
stchumers	idiots
stottit	staggered, bounced
stour	dust
Symon, Scot	Rangers manager, sacked suddenly
thrang	crowded
thrapple	throat, windpipe
tig	touch
tim	empty
Toshy	Charles Rennie Mackintosh
Tully, Charlie	Celtic footballer
wabbit	weak, fatigued
weans	children
wheecht	whipped
wheen	number
wimplin	winding
wulkies, tummle thur	somersault (tumble like wildcats)

INDEX OF POETS

MacDIARMID, Hugh (C.M. Grieve) 1892-1978
  from Glasgow *37*
  Glasgow, 1960 *35*
  In Glasgow *33*

MacDOUGALL, Carl b.1941 Glasgow
  Cod Liver Oil and Orange Juice *49*

McGINN, Matt d.1977 b. Glasgow
  The Butchers of Glasgow *134*

McGRATH, Tom b.1940 Rutherglen
  By Kelvin Water *96*
  Maryhill *145*
  "there was that time charlie tully" *111*

McLELLAN, Neil b.1954
  This Unrung Bell *134*

McNAUGHTAN, Adam
  The Jeely Piece Song *75*

MILTON, Jean b.1949
  the docks on Sunday *77*
  Glasgow   coming home again *118*

MONTGOMERIE, William b.1904 Glasgow
  Glasgow Street *34*
  Parkhead Cross *109*

MORGAN, Edwin b.1920 Glasgow
  At Central Station *144*
  By the Preaching of the Word *117*
  Glasgow Green *55*
  Glasgow Sonnets *91*
  G.M. Hopkins in Glasgow *155*
  In Glasgow *84*
  King Billy *54*
  Night Pillion *41*
  On John Maclean *115*
  Rider *79*
  The Starlings in George Square *51*
  To Joan Eardley *50*
  Trio *58*

FURTHER READING

Eyre-Todd (George)   *The Glasgow Poets: their lives and poems.* Glasgow & Edinburgh: William Hodge, 1903. 2nd edition, Paisley: Alexander Gardner, 1906.

Quigley (Hugh) *ed.*   *Lanarkshire in prose and verse.* Elkin Mathews & Marrot, 1929. (Sections on Glasgow and the Clyde).

Smith (David)   "The writers in Glasgow". *Glasgow University Magazine* 82:2, February 1971, p.22-23.

Glasgow University Magazine 82:3, 1971. Poetry Glasgow issue.

McGrath (Tom)   "The new Glasgow poets". *Glasgow Review* III:1, Summer 1972, p.17-22.

Akros 9: 25, August 1974. Glasgow issue.

Checkland (S.G.)   *The Upas Tree: Glasgow 1875-1975, a study in growth and contraction.* Glasgow: University of Glasgow Press, 1976. 2nd ed. 1981.

Oasis, 1:3, 1976.   Glasgow issue.

Glen (Duncan)   "Flourishing poetry in Glasgow and the west". *Styx* Spring 1976. (Glasgow College of Technology magazine)

Whyte (Hamish)   *Glasgow poets and poetry: a representative bibliography 1950-1975.* Glasgow, 1976. (Typescript in The Mitchell Library, Glasgow).

Thomson (Geddes) *ed.*   *Identities: an anthology of West of Scotland poetry, prose and drama.* Heinemann, 1981.

Hamilton (Robin)   "Myself and Poetry". *Akros* 16:48, December 1981, pp. 50-52 (on the Glasgow poetry scene in the '60s).

Four Glasgow Poems.   Glasgow District Libraries, 1982. (Dougal Graham, John Mayne, Alexander Smith, William McGonagall)

Aitken (A.J.)   "Bad Scots: Some Superstitions about Scots Speech". *Scottish Language* 1, Autumn 1982, pp.30-44.

Morgan (Edwin)   "Glasgow Speech in Recent Scottish Literature". In forthcoming festschrift for David Murison, provisionally titled *Scotland and the Lowland Tongue* (Aberdeen University Press, 1983).

Muir (James Hamilton)	*Glasgow in 1901.* William Hodge, 1901. With drawings by Muirhead Bone.
Bone (Muirhead)	*Fifty Drawings of Glasgow.* Maclehose, 1911.
Brogan (Colm)	*The Glasgow Story.* Muller, 1952. (With pictorial aids by Harry Keir).
Oakley (C.A.)	*The Second City.* 3rd ed. Blackie, 1975. (Lavishly illustrated).
Corrance (Douglas)	*Glasgow* (photographed by Douglas Corrance with commentary by Edward Boyd). Collins, 1981.

Hamish Whyte: born Giffnock, Glasgow, 1947. Educated at Hutchesons' Boys' Grammar School and Glasgow University (Honours degree in Classics). Currently Senior Librarian, Rare Books and Manuscripts Department, the Mitchell Library. Married, with two children, Kenneth and Christina, and lives in Glasgow.

Publications include: *apple on an orange day: poems* (Autolycus, 1973), *Siva in Lamlash: Arran Poems* (forthcoming, Arran Gallery Press); edited *Lady Castlehill's Receipt Book* (Molendinar, 1976) and *Edwin Morgan: a selected bibliography 1950-1980* (Mitchell Library, 1980). Poems in: *Akros, Cencrastus, Grand Piano, Palantir, Scottish Review, Words,* etc.

Is a partner in The Mariscat Press and co-editor of *The Glasgow Magazine.*

Cordelia Oliver: born and educated, Glasgow. Glasgow School of Art 1940-45. Art critic *Glasgow Herald* 1960-65. Writes regularly about Art and Theatre in *The Guardian, Sunday Standard, Plays Players.* Responsible for many exhibitions including: Jessie M. King, Joan Eardley, Painters in Parallel, 7 Scottish Artists, James Cowie, and Jack Knox.

ACKNOWLEDGEMENTS

Acknowledgements are due to the following magazines where many of the poems first appeared: *Akros, Aquarius, Cencrastus, Lines Review, New Edinburgh Review.*

For permission to reprint copyright material the editor and publishers gratefully acknowledge the following: Tom Berry for "Gorbals" and "In Memoriam — Anderston"; Tom Buchan for "Glasgow Sabbath"; Ronald Butlin and EUSPB for "The City Cemetery"; Stewart Conn and Hutchinson & Co. (Publishers) Ltd for "Arrivals", "Family Visit" and "A Sense of Order"; Catherine Lucy Czerkawska and Akros Publications for "Angles"; Andrew Fergus for "The Yairds" by his father J.F. Fergus; Ian Hamilton Finlay for "Glasgow Beasts, an a Burd"; EMI Music Publishing Ltd for Will Fyffe's "I Belong to Glasgow" (chorus), © 1921 Francis Day & Hunter Ltd; Duncan Glen for "Discovery", "The Hert o the City" and "Sweet Clyde"; Martin Brian & O'Keeffe for Iain Hamilton's "News of the World"; Nora Hunter (via Bette Stevenson) for "Lament for a Lost Dinner Ticket" by her mother Margaret Hamilton; Robin Hamilton for "The Girl I Met in Byres Road"; Cliff Hanley for "The Glasgow Underground"; J.F. Hendry and Borderline Press for "The Broomielaw" and "Glaschu"; Alan Jackson for "glasgow's full of artists"; T.M. Kirk for "Glasgow Types" and "Ode to the Clyde" by his father C.J. Kirk; Tom Leonard for "Six Glasgow Poems"; Maurice Lindsay and Robert Hale Ltd for "Glasgow Nocturne" and Maurice Lindsay for "Seen Out"; Liz Lochhead for "The Bargain", "Something I'm Not", "Obituary" and "Fetch on the First of January"; Kevin McCarra for "The Mitchell Library"; Louise McCorkindale and family for "School Friend" by her father Bill McCorkindale; Valda Grieve and Martin Brian & O'Keeffe for "Glasgow", "Glasgow, 1960" and "In Glasgow" by Hugh MacDiarmid; Carl MacDougall for "Cod Liver Oil and Orange Juice"; Janette McGinn for "The Butchers of Glasgow" by Matt McGinn; Tom McGrath for "By Kelvin Water", "Maryhill" and "there was that time charlie tully"; Neil McLellan for "This Unrung Bell"; Adam McNaughtan for "The Jeely Piece Song"; Jean Milton for "the docks on Sunday" and "Glasgow coming home"; William Montgomerie for "Glasgow Street" and "Parkhead Cross"; Edwin Morgan and Carcanet New Press Ltd for "At Glasgow Central", "Glasgow Green", "Glasgow Sonnets", "In Glasgow", "King Billy", "On John Maclean", "Rider", "The Starlings in George Square", "To Joan Eardley," "Trio" and Edwin Morgan for "By the Preaching of the Word", "G.M. Hopkins in Glasgow" and "Night Pillion"; Gavin Muir and Mainstream Publishing Co. (Edinburgh) Ltd for "The women talk . . ." by Edwin Muir; Stephen Mulrine and Carcanet New Press Ltd for "A Gude Buke" and Stephen Mulrine and Akros Publications for "The Coming of the Wee Malkies" and "Nostalgie"; Robin Munro for "Charing Cross"; David Neilson and the Mariscat Press for "Brindisi"; Alasdair Robertson for "A Song for Glasgow"; Alexander Scott and Akros Publications for "Glasgow Gangs" and Alexander Scott for "Rain in Sauchiehall Street"; Macdonald Publishers for "Glasgow" and "You Lived in Glasgow" by Iain Crichton Smith; Alan Spence for "Jingle"; Anne Stevenson and Carcanet New Press Ltd for "'Tiny Tunes Rule All'"; Jonathan Cape Ltd for "Glasgow Night" by Kenneth White; Hamish Whyte for "Gasometer Follies"; Tom Wright for "This is my Story".

Every effort has been made to secure permission to include the poems in this anthology; the editor and publishers apologize for any errors or omissions in the above and would be grateful to be notified of any corrections.

Thanks are due to the following for their kind permission to reproduce their work and works from their collections in this anthology:

Aberdeen Art Gallery *(page 29)*; T. and R. Annan and Sons; Mrs James Black *(Eardley colour plates)*; J.D. Fergusson Foundation; Ian Fleming RSA; John Gilmour; Glasgow Museums and Art Galleries *(6, 30, 145)*; Alasdair Gray; Imperial War Museum *(Spencer colour plates)*; R. Jennings *(Whone colour plate)*; John Kraska; Bet Low; Tom MacDonald; Pete McGinn; Oscar Marzaroli; James Miller; James Morrison; Graham Murray; Ken Murray; People's Palace *(17 bottom, 26)*; John Picking; Willie Rodger; Professor Andrew Sykes; Margaret Watt; and Herbert Whone.

The Pope's helicopter landing. Bellahouston Park, 1982. Glasgow Herald

176 The start of the Glasgow Marathon, Tron Steeple, 1983. Glasgow Herald

Glasgow tramcar in fog. Oil on board, 1961. Herbert Whone

The Dome; Botanic Gardens. Oil on canvas, 1953. J.D. Fergusson

Kirklee Bridge. Oil on canvas, 1941. J.D. Fergusson

Garnethill. Oil on canvas, 1955. Bet Low

Sauchiehall Street with Unity Theatre. Oil on canvas, c1947. Bet Low

Gable-end mural, Garnethill, 1978. John Kraska

High tea, Ruchazie, 1979. Margaret Watt

Air raid shelters in a tenement lane. Etching, 1942. Ian Fleming

Troop ships on the Clyde, 1947. Mitchell Library

Prior to launching, John Brown's Shipyard, 1960. Oscar Marzaroli

Hopper on the Clyde, near Colville's Ore Terminal, 1965. Oscar Marzaroli

The Template (detail), Port Glasgow. Oil on canvas, completed May 1942. Sir Stanley Spencer

Burners (detail), Port Glasgow. Oil on canvas, completed Autumn 1940. Sir Stanley Spencer

Riggers (detail), Port Glasgow. Oil on canvas, completed June 1944. Sir Stanley Spencer

Plumbers (detail), Port Glasgow. Oil on canvas, completed March 1945. Sir Stanley Spencer

Gorbals Church from Clyde Street. Oil on canvas, 1953. Tom Macdonald

Port Dundas. Oil on board, 1947. Bet Low

Two kids scribbling on a wall. Gouache, c.1955. Joan Eardley

Glasgow school children enjoying a Scottish Opera workshop, Third Eye Centre, 1979.
George Oliver

Athole Gardens. Oil on canvas, 1964. James Morrison ARSA

Shields Road, 1982. George Oliver

Park Terrace, 1983. George Oliver

Morning light, Kelvingrove Park, 1960. Oscar Marzaroli

Gorbals skyline, 1964. Oscar Marzaroli

Gorbals tenements and Southern Necropolis, 1964. Oscar Marzaroli

:addens, 1950. Oil on board, 1964. Alasdair Gray

Tenement and washing. Pastel, c.1955. Joan Eardley

Back street: children playing. Oil on board, c.1955. Joan Eardley

Three girls at a tenement window. Gouache, c.1955. Joan Eardley